HOW ARE BABIES MADE?
WHAT DOES IT MEAN TO BE GAY?
DO YOU HAVE TO BE MARRIED TO MAKE A BABY? WHAT IS AIDS?

Questions about sex and sexuality continually perplex children from generation to generation. Husband-and-wife counseling team Leon and Barbara Somers, who specialize in working with families and are parents themselves, know that an open and trusting relationship between parent and child is often the key to preventing such problems as sexual abuse, teen pregnancy, and sexually transmitted diseases. This warm and reassuring guide offers both stimulating quizzes and true-to-life dialogues, giving parents the information and the confidence they need to educate children about sex — and its all-important relationship to love.

"TEACHES PARENTS HOW TO CONVEY TO THEIR CHILDREN THE ACCEPTANCE AND SENSITIVITY THAT HELPS INSTILL HEALTHY ATTITUDES ABOUT LOVE AND SEX."
—Marianne Neifert, M.D., author of *Doctor Mom*

LEON AND BARBARA SOMERS are a husband-and-wife counseling team. They run the Somers Trust, a psychological service center in North Andover, Massachusetts, where they practice individual, family, marital, and group therapy and act as consultants to the courts, business, and industry. They have three grown children.

Talking to Your Children About Love and Sex

LEON SOMERS, Ed.D.,
and
BARBARA C. SOMERS, M.Ed.

A SIGNET BOOK

SIGNET
Published by the Penguin Group
Penguin Books USA Inc., 375 Hudson Street,
New York, New York 10014, U.S.A.
Penguin Books Ltd, 27 Wrights Lane,
London W8 5TZ, England
Penguin Books Australia Ltd, Ringwood,
Victoria, Australia
Penguin Books Canada Ltd, 2801 John Street,
Markham, Ontario, Canada L3R 1B4
Penguin Books (N.Z.) Ltd, 182–190 Wairau Road,
Auckland 10, New Zealand

Penguin Books Ltd, Registered Offices:
Harmondsworth, Middlesex, England

Talking to Your Children About Love and Sex previously appeared
in an NAL Books edition.

First Signet Printing, May, 1990
10 9 8 7 6 5 4 3 2 1

REGISTERED TRADEMARK—MARCA REGISTRADA

Printed in the United States of America

To our children
and
To Kerry and Todd

Acknowledgments

It is with gratitude and humility that we acknowledge the contributions to this book. To begin with, our children started us on our educational path with their own observations, experiments, and experiences. Their friends and children added to the process. Our friends' encouragement and support were certainly inspirational as we wrote this book.

Our literary agent, Ruth Wreschner, recognized our work and promoted it. We are grateful for her wise guidance through the complexities of publication.

Our editor, Alexia Dorszynski, proved to be another experienced guide who provided very informed suggestions and enormous help.

And finally, our typist Frances Jennings, provided typing services and critical comments to which we paid great attention.

Our thanks to all, with special appreciation to our daughter Jo Ann for her professional guidance.

Contents

Talking to Your Children About Love and Sex

INTRODUCTION

Talking to Children About Love and Sex

We recognize that parents have always known it was important to talk to their children about sex. Yet we have always had a hard time doing so. Why should that be? Well, for one good reason, most of us never had a model to go by. Our parents generally didn't provide us with much information, and, as a result, we felt we could never depend on them to answer our questions. For another, we learned what we needed to one way or another, and *we're* okay—after all, we produced the next generation. But while that's indisputably true, what each generation has lost in this process is the chance to become truly intimate, to develop the kind of trust that bonds one generation to another and provides an immeasurable richness.

The kind of intimacy we're discussing cannot be generated from classroom teaching, although most schools do provide some sort of sex education for young people so that, by the time they graduate from high school, most children should have a clear idea about human reproduction. They will be in much better shape than the mother of one woman we know, who fifty years ago, had had a hysterectomy but continued to worry about preventing further births. Our friend's poor mother hadn't connected the removal of her uterus with her ability to have children. The mother herself was one of six children and a high school graduate. Clearly, neither her mother nor her school had been of much help to her in terms of information about reproduction. But now most schools do teach sex education, so any high school graduate should know better than our friend's mother. So what's left for us as parents?

What's left for us as parents is the opportunity to model trust and intimacy with our children. In an age where the sexual abuse of our young is an acknowledged fact and teenage pregnancy, venereal diseases, and now AIDS provide another ugly reality, it is more important than ever that we talk to our youngsters about sex and about safety, and about love—not just for their own information and safety but because we want to establish a relationship with them that makes it clear that parents can be trusted to be supportive, available, and a good resource for them to turn to if they face different decisions or problems.

There are lots of excellent books available that are packed with information about telling children about sex, but we have yet to find one that demonstrates how to use the information appropriately. What we want is to make it possible for you to talk to your child comfortably, rather than assign him a book to read. And so we have developed dialogues for use with children of all ages to demonstrate the kinds of questions children ask and the kinds of answers that satisfy them. In this way, you can prepare yourself by seeing how it can be done. We have tried to imagine scenarios where both parents are involved in the discussion, where a mother talks to a daughter, a mother talks to a son, or a father talks to a daughter or son. In other words, we have tried to anticipate every configuration—from single parent to coupled parents—in which parents talk to their children.

For the sake of equality between the genders, we have alternated the use of the pronouns *he* and *she*. In the Introduction and in Chapter One we have used *he*. In Chapter Two we have used *she*, and so on. When we explore gender-specific issues such as pregnancy, or wet dreams, we suspend the rule for the sake of clarity.

We have traced the sexual development of the child from

birth through adolescence, providing information as well as guidance in the form of dialogues about teaching your child about sex and answering all his questions in a comfortable, natural way. And, of course, we also explore the development of love and the many forms it takes as our children mature.

It may seem strange to consider love as developmental, but it certainly is. Your child grows from self-centeredness as an infant to a bonding with a parent to an awareness of and joining with other family members. Then he goes on to invest in friends, groups, and finally partners. It is an important journey, one that should be nourished and fostered. When we speak of a well-adjusted person, in large measure we are talking about a person who can reach out to others in trust and love. That person has *learned* to love successfully.

It is important to know that whether you answer each and every one of your child's questions accurately each and every time is immaterial. You can always go back and correct mistakes. It's a human thing to do, after all. But what is vital is that your child will know that he can trust you to be interested and available for his intimate concerns. That's a rare and precious gift, which both you and your child deserve.

We also help you on a journey through your own sexual history so that you have a clearer idea of how your own sexual philosophy was formulated.

As to who *we* are: We are both psychotherapists with over twenty years in practice. We are the founders of a clinic that deals with families, and we have paid particular attention to parenting. Both of us are also sex therapists and marriage counselors; this has provided us with a rich assortment of experiences from which to draw our examples.

We have worked with single parents, divorced parents, stepparents, gay parents, and just about every combination and permutation imaginable. We have seen them struggle to bring up their children, and we have shared that struggle with them.

We have also both been teachers, with experience ranging from elementary school to college and graduate level. We have done radio and television broadcasting, and it seems that we have lectured in most of the church basements and school auditoriums within fifty miles of our home.

As psychotherapists, educators, parents, and grandparents, we have shared the adventure of trying to find intimacy and love with our children.

CHAPTER ONE

Learning to Love

How Do Our Children Learn to Love?

One of the most thrilling events that happens in parents' relationship with their children occurs when they realize that their children's smiles and hugs are for them alone. As parents, we recall the anxiety and concern we felt for our newborn, and we also realize that his primary needs are for food and shelter—which anyone can provide. But when a child singles us out for a smile but scowls at strangers, then we really know he's as bonded as we are. About the time those two front teeth of his appear, we know we're a family with mutual investments in each other. His preference for us is one of our best rewards for those sleepless nights—it's clear that the work is all worthwhile.

But much as we love his love, we're constantly helping him to expand his loving. We introduce key characters in glowing terms. "Here's Grandma," we crow; "say Nana." Without realizing it, we are teaching our children to expand the number of people they love, and to reach out and be warm and friendly. And we can count on delighted grandparents, close relatives, and friends to reassure our baby that he is indeed special and worthy of love. It's love begetting love and trust.

As our child grows older and more trusting, he begins to make neighborhood and nursery school friends, but home is where his security lies and will for a long time. But, at the same time, he is perfectly willing to have a friend to play with for a few hours, and he is perfectly willing to go to school for a few hours. Again, we encourage his expanding love and trust by encouraging him to increase his group of loved ones. By the time he is three or four, he may even be willing to spend a night away from home with a trusted grandparent or close friend. A little girl may be ready to spend the night at a friend's house—but at seven the next morning she may call her mother to see if she will come over and fix her braids. Other adults may be as willing, if not as proficient as her mother, but she needs that security, even at six. Once she has seen her mommy, she may be content to spend the rest of the day. She is willing to reach out so long as she knows home base is still there.

By the time children enter first grade, they're pretty social. They may still hang their heads and mutter a "hello" when they are introduced to strangers but, nonetheless, they are in the process of selecting "best" friends, as well as other friends who interest them. Those interests can be based on odd phenomena—a child may be fascinated and then devoted to another student who has broken an arm. Parents will be treated to daily medical bulletins about the progress of this new friend. As the arm improves and finally is released from its cast, however, the child's intense interest may dry up. The poor friend will lose her singularity and thus her appeal.

By the time children are eight or so, groups become important. Scouting activities, team sports, after-school groups, are now where they want to be. The best friend has generally expanded into a group of favorites. As parents, we've done our work well. Our child has continued to expand and grow in sociability and friendship. That, of course, is one of our parenting goals: to have a child who can move comfortably in a group and trust the group to treat him cordially. But always our love and support are the fuel for our child's emotional motor.

This is also the time when our daughters arrive home flushed and excited because the boys have been chasing them in the schoolyard. It may also be a time of snatched kisses and teasing, gifts—a ball or a frog—and telephone calls. It's incredible that Romeo and Juliet got so much accomplished without the aid of the telephone, which now begins to resemble some new kind of umbilical cord.

As our children move on to junior high, they begin to have crushes that can be pretty intense as well as short-lived. They also find mentors. This is a time of hero worship. Girls as well as boys often turn to coaches, or single out particular teachers for intense relationships. As parents we may begin to become uncomfortably aware that we have some shortcomings. We are not the super-parents our children's adoration had taught us we were. Now what Mr. Martin says, or Ms. Murphy says, has greater importance and validity than what we say. This is the time for one parent to mutter to the other, "Maybe Mr. Martin can convince Billy to take out the trash."

As parents, we can also remember our own progression from what others called "puppy love"—we know it was the real thing—to more serious and intense affairs until we finally selected the one who made bells ring and stars shine. We remember whether our parents were critical or understanding, mocking or sympathetic, interested or indifferent. We remember the pain of wrong choices and how comforting it was if our parents could acknowledge that they'd had hard times, too.

We also have made the journey from early sexual play, to the excitement of kissing games, to the challenge of friends urging us to headier experiments, to our first sexual experience. What we realize is that nothing compares with the total joy of responsible sex and love. We would like our children to learn that, too.

We can be there for our children because we've been there, too. And we can share with them because we know that the most precious gift we have to give and to receive is that of love. That's really what we want our children to know as they awaken sexually.

So how do we parents get this double job done—teaching our kids about love and sex and how they go together? What can we do to help ourselves be good teachers and models? Is it all words and ideas, or is there something we can concretely *do*?

In fact there are two things we can do—two things with which we can struggle, might be a better way to put it. These two tasks may seem simple, but they demand patience, persistence, and insight. They are:

- Determining our own sexual beliefs and standards.
- Understanding our own sexual history.

Your Attitudes About Love and Sex

We'll start with sexual beliefs and standards. We might call these your sexual philosophy. We want you to get in touch with your own ideas about sex so that you can say what you believe to your children in simple, direct terms. If you can put your ideas into words, you will have a better understanding of what those ideas are, be able to teach them clearly, and be able to respond constructively to the curves kids frequently pitch *at* you.

Consider, for example, what happened when twenty-one-year-old Jennifer came home for Christmas vacation from her senior year at college. She had asked her parents if she might bring Eddie with her. They had readily agreed because they had met Eddie a few times and approved of the relationship. Jennifer's parents knew she and Ed were deeply in love and were planning marriage. What they did not know was that Jennifer planned to have Ed sleep with her in her room at home. "You know we often stay together overnight when we are at school—we have been doing that for over two years now. So why can't we do it here?"

Her parents had indeed known. They had had a long talk about it and had some difference of opinion. Her father felt that as long as Jennifer was cautious, responsible, and monogamous, it was something they had to accept. "After all," he said, "they are a thousand miles away from us and we have no actual control or power." Jennifer's mother had reluctantly accepted that reality, but when it came to *her home* she knew what she wanted, and knew she had the power to enforce it. After her husband agreed to support her position she stated that position clearly to Jennifer and Ed together. "I want you both to know that I have certain standards for my children in my house, and one of those standards is that there will be no sex before marriage between these walls. Your father and I have agreed to this. Ed, you may sleep in the family room downstairs and agree to stay there alone all night every night, or we will get you a nice room in the motel downtown."

Tough lady? Maybe so—but Jennifer and Ed knew what the limits and alternatives were and were free to make their choices. They also knew that they were not put down, that their different standards were accepted on their turf, but not accepted on Jennifer's mother's. They were not devalued, called names, or subjected to a wrenching argument about standards and beliefs. They also knew that Dad was in agreement and they could not try to manipulate him, even though his beliefs might have differed.

That's an example of why we want you to know and be able to say where you stand on sexual issues. We have found that you will be more comfortable teaching and talking about sex with your children if you first explore the many things you automatically presume, then make them conscious and verbal. We want you to understand, for example, what it means to you to be a man or a woman, how you feel about your body, how you were taught about sex, not only by direct instruction but also by observing other people's sexual beliefs and behaviors.

Let's clarify what we mean by beliefs and behaviors. *Behavior* means everyday acts like staying clothed around the house and locking the bathroom door. (We knew one family who were "liberal" and did not install bathroom doors in their new home—until the building inspector refused to grant permit for occupancy without those doors!) *Beliefs* include things like equality of the sexes, "double standards," or sexual fidelity.

As an example, let's consider a sexual standard that arises very early: As a teenager, how did you feel about the difference between boys and girls? Did you feel that boys were more likely to "do it" than girls? If you did, then were girls somehow "purer" than boys? If you did, then it would also follow that you saw boys as being able to take "purity" away from girls. Girls were sexual victims and boys were sexual aggressors.

So now you are a parent and you have a beautiful daughter. Our idea is that with a standard like the example in the preceding paragraph, it would be reasonable to expect that you would be protective of your daughter. You might caution her about boys and their dangerous sexual tendencies. You might limit her exposure to boys. You might even go so far as to send her to an all-girls school. You might not even realize why you chose that school, and emphasize that you chose it because of its excellent teaching. While all this is going on, is your message to your daughter that she is vulnerable where boys are concerned and had better watch it?

Let's run our fantasy out a bit further. Daughter, let's call her Dorothy, is a gutsy kid and decides she will show you she can take care of herself just fine. She is fourteen, just getting home from school one afternoon, and says to her mother:

Dorothy: I'm going out for a while, Mom, be back about five.
Mother: What about your homework, dear?
Dorothy: I'll have plenty of time. So long.

Mother: Just a minute, Dorothy, where are you going?

Dorothy: Just out, to see the kids.

Mother: Kids, what kids?

Dorothy: Oh, Amy, Billy, Sue—you know, the gang.

Mother: Yes, I know about Billy all right. I don't want you playing with him alone.

Dorothy: Mother! What's wrong with Billy? All the kids like him—he's cute.

Mother: That's just the point. I've heard about him—

Dorothy: Mom, cut it out, please. You are always hearing about boys, and this is the only chance I have to know the kids on my own street.

And so it goes. Dorothy is turned off by her mother's suspicion. We can imagine that perhaps she will secretly see boys, or that she will seek her father's support against her mother, or in some way act out against her mother's sexual beliefs. We may be oversimplifying things in this example but our point is obvious: We want you as a parent to understand and know your beliefs so that old, automatic habits won't get in the way of helping kids come to grips with sexual feelings.

Let's consider how you feel about men being "macho"— aggressive and dictatorial—or "manly," and how that relates to your style as a sex model for your kids. In your view, should males be macho or manly in their attitude toward sex and the performance of sex? Does that mean that men "lead" in sexual approaches and actions? "A manly man initiates sex." He directs it and is in charge of the scenario. He might do that gently or roughly, but he is the one in charge. Should women expect that? Are you going to teach your daughter to expect it, put up with it, or resist it? Are you going to teach your son to take that stance?

It's clear that a common idea like men being manly has many meanings and consequences for one's whole sexual life. If you agree with it, you might be teaching chauvinism to boys and submission to girls. If you disagree with it, you may be doing the opposite or be fostering equality of the sexes. Those are important messages to be sending to kids— and you should recognize that you're sending them!

Your Sexual Beliefs and Standards

We'd like to make one thing clear in this discussion. We are *not* trying to influence your attitudes about sex in one way or another. Our interest and purpose is not to foster liberalism or conservatism, or any other "ism." We just want you to identify *your* sexual preferences so that you know what they are, understand them, and understand how they might influence your child.

Let's try something together. We'll propose a list of questions. Take a piece of paper and put it beside the questions, making at least three columns for the answers you will write in beside the questions. Head the first column "Agree/Disagree" (Yes/No), and the second column, "Probable Effect on Children." Make a third column headed "Feeling." Your sheet will look something like this (make the columns wider than we can show on this page—you'll need the space).

Question	Agree/Disagree (Yes/No)	Probable Effect on Children	Feeling

We will suggest some questions to start you off. As you go through them, you'll think of questions that are probably more relevant to your own life than ours could ever be. Write them down and try to respond to them. They will be the real bonus to this effort.

Some of our questions may not fit the format too well, but think about your answers. If the question arouses a feeling in you—such as anger or frustration or sadness—write that down, too. It's important. Now, here are the questions.

- Do you support women's rights?
- Should women invite and initiate sex?
- Have you changed your position on this question as the years have passed?
- If you have changed, will you tell your child you did?
- Will he or she learn flexibility from that?
- Should girls be feminine and frilly?
- Does being "sexy" destroy a woman's feminity?
- Does it cheapen her?
- How does a woman's style of sexuality affect men? Shy men? Bold men?
- Will you recommend any particular style of sexuality to your daughter?
- Should she develop her own style?
- Will you let her know if you approve or disapprove?
- Are women's sexual rights more recognized than when you were a child?
- Does the Pill change women's sexual rights?
- Does the threat of AIDS change women's sexual rights?
- Are men more understanding of a woman's risk of pregnancy since the discovery of AIDS because they now face risk of fatal disease?
- Are women responsible for contraception?
- Have you changed your sexual standards since the discovery of AIDS?
- If so, are you more conservative?
- Do you want to encourage your child to be conservative about sex?

- Do girls who are popular at school adjust to sex more easily than girls who are not popular?
- Do popular boys automatically like sex?
- Are popular girls more likely to marry and have families or to remain single and become career women?
- Are popular boys more likely to become "swinging bachelors"?
- Does self-esteem play a part in sexual development?
- Can fat girls say no?
- Should fat boys date only fat girls?
- Are shy boys "safer" for girls to date?
- Are homely girls more of a "pushover"?
- Do you believe in a democratic relationship between men and women?
- Do you project or model such a relationship to your kids?
- Does your spouse or lover support or undermine that?
- Do you have a lock on your bedroom door?
- Should children know if their parents make love?
- Do you believe in the "double standard"—that men can be promiscuous but women should not?
- Would you prefer your daughter to be a virgin when she marries?
- How about your son?
- Would you prefer that your children live with someone before getting married?
- Have your opinions on the above group of questions changed since you were a child?
- Do you expect your children might make similar changes in their sexual attitudes as their life goes on?
- Is whatever two consenting adults do sexually okay?

- What about two consenting adolescents?
- If you had it to do over, what would you change about your adolescent sexual behavior?
- Would you discuss that with your adolescent child?

Those are heavy questions, and there are many of them. Actually, they are only a sample of the hundreds of questions people must explore in order to clarify their own sexual attitudes.

Let's look at some of the responses we have heard in our practices and what those responses might mean to parents who were learning about themselves to better instruct their children about love and sex.

Geraldine is forty years old. She said that women should indeed invite and initiate sex, but only with their husbands. When we asked her how she felt about that answer, she said she felt "assertive." She had indeed changed her position on this question—about eight years earlier. She planned to tell her child that she had changed her point of view and that her child would see that as a model of flexible adaptation. She did not feel that being "sexy" destroyed her femininity, so long as she was only sexy with her husband. To behave otherwise would cheapen her in any other man's eyes. She felt that starting to take the Pill coincided with her change to initiating sex. Geraldine was very comfortable with her ideas until we asked a question that seemed to suit her context: "At what age would you like to see your daughter start taking the Pill?"

She sat bolt upright, looked around the room searchingly for a moment, and said, "When she gets married, of course. What do you mean, 'at what age'?" We asked her how she felt about that last question, and she replied that she was annoyed by it—and then burst out laughing. "I guess I am struggling between a newer sexual freedom and my older ideas, the ones I was brought up to believe. Do you think my daughter would pick that up?" We had met her daughter. She had already picked that up.

Let's talk about Stuart. He is a little younger—about thirty-five. He believes in a democratic relationship between men and women. He says he lives it: He shares cooking and washing duties and is an equal partner in taking care of the kids. "Love to cook, especially weekends when I can create." He and his wife have no trouble splitting the household tasks. He insists on a lock on the bedroom door and is sure the kids know why. He frequently tells them openly that they are not to disturb Mom and Dad for an hour.

He would like his daughter to be a virgin when she marries—but, no, it does not matter if his son is or isn't. His son can live with someone before he gets married, but he is sure his wife would not go to visit them in their home. *He* would. He wishes he had been born twenty-five years later, and he sure would have changed his behavior as an adolescent. No more "choir boy" stuff for him. He wishes he had given and accepted as many invitations as possible.

Stuart's ambivalence is clear: He lives democracy on the household level but subscribes to the double standard on a sexual level. Geraldine knows she is struggling, and will be open about that struggle with her daughter. Can you imagine what effect their attitudes will have on their childrens' sexuality?

Understanding Our Own Sexual history

Just as our sexual beliefs and standards underlie what we will be teaching our children, so our sexual history affects the automatic sexual behavior we demonstrate in our daily lives. When Lydia was a child, her mother always yelled at father to "Put some clothes on!" as he came sauntering out of the marital bedroom with just his shorts on. He never slept with anything on, disdaining pajamas for the cool feeling of elegant sheets, and being readily available, without encumberance for any sexual eventuality that might, he hoped, occur that night. Lydia's mother, on the other hand, was always elegantly covered with safe and silky nightgowns. Lydia's father would not tolerate pajamas on his wife. When her mother emerged from the bedroom, even half asleep and disheveled, she represented swishy propriety with a hint of healthy, sexual availability.

Father was affectionate with his daughter and, if she came into the bedroom while he was in bed, she got warm cuddles—with the sheet carefully kept between them. This was usually accompanied by Mother's perturbed complaints, half-whispered, half-chirped, that he be sure to stay covered, and that Lydia really ought to go take her morning bath. We don't know what will happen to Lydia—we hope she'll identify with her father and be healthy.

Reaching back in your memory for sexual history is sometimes rather difficult. Those memories are sensitive and may be hard to reach. You may have trouble with recall, but try to remember, and don't be discouraged if it takes a few tries. You may profit from some help from family or friends who knew you when you were a child and can tell some stories you might not have heard before. If you have siblings, you are indeed fortunate because you can compare and contrast how each of you was treated by your parents.

Perhaps the most fun of all is to see how different your memories are. You will be amazed at how you might differ about the same events and what they signified to you. Lydia's brother, for example, might have remembered his father as a stubborn old fool who slept naked just to annoy his mother, who was rather prudish. Thus can human understandings be compared to a two-edged blade wielded by a Monday morning quarterback.

As you read on, you might want to have beside you a sheet of paper similar to the last one we suggested. This time the headings might read:

Question	Probable Effect on Children	Feeling

As we recommended earlier, add your own memories to those we suggest; they will be very important ones for you to work with.

Start with the earliest memories you have of being a child. Get back to babyhood if you can. Try to recall being held: Who held you the most? Who did not hold you? Who was your favorite "holder"? Were you cuddled? By whom? Were there special occasions for cuddling? Did your mother and father take you into their bed for cuddles? Was there a special time, like Saturday morning, when you could run into their room and jump into bed with them?

One of our clients, whom we will call Ben, had a special memory of similar events. He got up early Saturdays and tried to sneak out of the big double bed where he slept with his sister. He was five, and she was nine. He was one of four children crowded into a small apartment, so he slept with his sister—for the time being. He hated it, and hated her, especially when, on Saturday mornings, she would inevitably spoil his fun cuddling with Mom and Dad. She did it by jumping on their bed to join in the fun. She was big for her age, and very fat, and inevitably the mattress slipped through the cold wooden slats and everybody landed on the floor. Everybody laughed except Ben, who howled in anger at the abrupt end of *his* special attention time.

Why had Ben come to see us? Because he and his wife of five years were buying their first house, refurnishing their bedroom, and she was insisting on a king-size bed to replace the twin beds given to them by her parents. Ben was equally insistent that they replace the old twin beds with two new ones. His wife, of course, was slightly overweight. We asked him what feelings the earlier events led him to recall. He remembered feeling warm, happy, scared, and later, wistful. He left anger out of the list, until we reminded him.

Let's go back to work on memories. Can you remember who dressed you as a child? Were you made aware that your clothes reflected whether you were a boy or a girl? Did someone praise you for looking pretty in your dress? For looking like a "little man" in your new pants and sweater? Those were all gender-training experiences from which you could learn which sex you were and act accordingly.

Who bathed you? Was it the parent of the same sex? Was it specifically either parent? Both? Was there someone you liked best to give you a bath or a shower? As you grew older, did you ask to bathe yourself alone? Did you feel like a big person when you did that? If you did, that was part of your growing sense of your own sexual identity. From those experiences you learned about your own comfort with yourself.

You might also have learned about it from watching your parents. For example: Think of the difference in your view of body privacy if, on the one hand, your parents were casual about being nude in the bathroom together and if, on the other hand, mother shouted whenever Dad accidentally opened the bathroom door. Those were sexual clues that will help you see yourself as relaxed or tense about nudity, perhaps.

When our first daughter was four, we had a bathroom event we will never forget. She had become fascinated with a story about a sheriff who protected the Old West in gun-toting style. She wanted a toy gun, and we bought it for her with some reluctance. We always left the bathroom doors unlocked so that we could be alerted to the usual child emergencies. I, the male member of this family, was toweling off after my shower, and was bent over my toes, rear end pointing toward the door. It opened, and with a shout of "Stick 'em up, BANG!" Lonnie vigorously applied the cold muzzle of her toy pistol—you know where! Now, thirty-five years later, Lonnie is fine but my wife complains about my locking the bathroom door when I shower . . .

Let's move your personal sexual history up to about eight years of age and explore the period from then to about the age of twelve—or whenever your body began to mature.

The clues you remember from this age will probably seem more directly relevant to your own sexual development. For example, did you play "doctor" and look at the genital areas of someone of the opposite sex? Probably you started with same-sexed friends because children of this age are pretty much interested only in their own sex. Perhaps you explored your own body first. Did you have the courage to get a mirror and look? If you did, did you feel a bit guilty? If you felt guilty, what did you do about that feeling?

Were you ever caught or found out? What happened? Were you punished or scolded? Were you made to feel that you were wicked, bad, or dirty? Think about your feelings and how you might have felt if treated differently. How would you now treat your child if you caught him in a similar situation?

We recall a couple of examples of such situations. One was Tom, age twenty-nine, who grinned as he told us how his father caught him kissing his cousin on the porch at age twelve. Dad ordered Tom off the porch and escorted little Sarah safely inside. Tom's father never mentioned it again, and Tom said he still wonders what Dad was thinking.

Doris, age thirty-seven, sobbed as she recalled her shame at her father calling her a whore and a slut because he found her kissing her date in the car when they came home from a dance. She had never asked her dates to come in—her father drank a lot and she could not predict what shape he would be in. Doris is now a sexually active woman, but cannot set limits for a man. She wonders if her daughter will have the same problem. Doris had lived with her alcoholic husband for twelve years and only instituted divorce proceedings after he had abandoned her and her children for two years.

Let's explore another stage of your own sexual history. This one is easier to remember, perhaps. For girls, that stage was, of course, the menarche—the beginning of menstruation. There has been a lot of thinking and writing about that stage; We'll spare you from rehashing it here, but do reach for the memory and then, most importantly, for the feelings you experienced then. Name them now; write them down. Perhaps when you talk to your daughter about menstruation, you can tell her about those feelings you had.

You who are mothers have probably decided how your presentation to your daughter will be different from the experience you had. If you were more fortunate in the way you were told, perhaps you hope to duplicate the *good* experience you had.

For the boys, this stage meant the beginning of nocturnal emissions, increased sensitivity to unexpected, unwanted, spontaneous erections, and the beginning of masturbation. We know, of course, that girls masturbate, too, but let's just consider the boys for a moment. Boys begin to grow pubic hair at about this time, and their voices change, sometimes in a most embarrassing way. When this happened to you, were you proud or ashamed? Did your family gently accept these changes with perhaps some kind kidding, or did they pretend to ignore it? Did your friends compare proof of masturbation with you in the locker room after gym? Were you one of the slow starters in your gang, or did you begin early and lead the others?

For boys or girls, early adolescence is a time of great sensitivity. Lesley, for instance, never got over the discomfort of large breasts. By the time she was twelve, she was the butt of cruel jokes and began to hang her head and walk round-shouldered. She had two older brothers who wanted to be "helpful" so they told her how women with large breasts were more likely to get breast cancer. Norma was different. At the age of thirteen, she was taller than most of the boys. She was proud of her ample bosom, and when the boys teased her, she laughed. If they went too far and got dirty, she belted them until they were silent.

Again, we see that the same condition can have different results for different people. Lesley's liability was Norma's asset. We wonder whether that difference orginated in the body messages their parents and families conveyed. Lesley certainly got negative stuff from her brothers. We don't have enough information about Norma, probably because we tend to explore unhealthy results retrospectively and don't pay enough attention to healthy histories.

Let's go forward a few years in your personal sexual history. Let's go to the years you might remember only too well: your first sexual experiences. Were *you* prepared? Had your parents, teachers, siblings, or friends adequately taught you what to expect? And, to make the question even more relevant, were you prepared for the *feelings* you experienced? Did you have people you trusted to whom you could talk about those feelings? Did you and your partner talk about how you felt? Would sharing feelings have helped? Might you have done the whole thing differently? Might someone have suggested more or less sex? If you had reconsidered and followed that suggestion, might your whole life have changed? Would you have married that person? Would you have had that child—at that time? Would you have had that abortion?

We talked with Fran when she was twenty-nine, married, with three children, burned out, and still trying to make a shaky marriage work. She said she never really knew what happened to her, but at sixteen she was pregnant. When she told her boyfriend, he responded responsibly. Ed was eighteen, out of high school, working as a mechanics helper in a repair shop, and he loved Fran dearly. They talked with their parents and both families agreed that the best thing for the kids was to get married. Fran would drop out of school at the end of her junior year, which was only three months away. Ed was the last child left at home in his house, and they could have his room. Fran could work and contribute toward expenses. Everybody accepted the inevitable and helped.

They lived with Ed's folks for two years, got their own little place, and with help from both families, managed to get along. With the children came responsibility, routine, lots of work, and boredom with each other. Too much work, too much togetherness, not enough fun, and absolutely no "marriage" time. Thirteen years passed without a vacation for Fran and Ed alone together. Until they talked with us, they had not even considered that couples might be entitled to vacations without their children being along.

When we got to feelings, it all poured out. Both felt so obligated by guilt that they did not feel entitled to any fun. They could accept joy—in their children and for their children. But that they should have *fun* would mean that they were accepting a reward for being sinful. That could never be! They must work, work, work.

Clearly, the sexual events in our history have done much to shape our lives. Carry your own history forward, now, at your own speed, but do try to do it thoroughly. You may find yourself having to skip certain parts, but they may come back to you as you go along. That is because as you review your own past, you'll probably be more accepting, and thus you will recall things you might have blocked the first time around. Perhaps a few days later you will recollect things you have forgotten for years. Be gentle with yourself. Some of these memories have been firmly buried under layers of defenses for years!

When you are finished—as if there is such a thing—take an open look at where you are now. Do you have a satisfactory sexual partner? Are you monogamous? Is your partner monogamous? Is your partner your spouse? Are you happy with the sexual life you share? Do you think your partner is sexually happy with you? Do you talk about it together? If not, what do you do about it? Do you think talking together will help as you teach your child about sex and love? Will your spouse or partner help in educating your child in a healthy way? Do you trust him or her to do that?

We know we have suggested some hard work for you. In this chapter we have talked about love, sexual beliefs and standards, and the pervasive effect of your own sexual history. We hope the work pays off for you as parents and for your children. We have seen it help others. Now, having studied yourselves, let's study the kids for a while.

CHAPTER TWO

How We Start:
From Birth to Five Years

How old should my child be before I begin talking to her about love and sex?

What should I tell my child about love and sex?

These are sensible questions frequently asked by conscientious parents. They look surprised when we say, "Well, you already have. You started the day he was born." And so you did. At the moment of birth you said, "Oh, good, a girl" or "Oh, good, a boy." The moment you saw your baby, you told her what her sex is. That is sexual information/gender identification. Of course, the baby understands none of this, but as parents you have already begun the process of naming and identifying in a very natural way.

Identification and explanation are the intellectual ways that parents teach children about sex. But there is another kind of sexual information that you provide to your children from the moment of birth that you mustn't lose sight of. The attitudinal information you give is just as important as the factual and it, too, begins at once. When you hold an infant tenderly and kiss, rock, cuddle, and hug him, you are showing him that holding, touching, and kissing are all pleasurable. Babies can't be held and kissed enough. There's nothing like a reassuring hug and kiss for little ones. Think of the routine you go through automatically. When your toddler falls and cries, what is your response? "Show me

24

where it hurts. I'll kiss it and make it all go away." You are teaching your little ones that kissing and hugging are not only pleasurable; they're also *magical*. They make the hurt all better.

You also teach them that being affectionate is a mark of respect and love. When relatives or friends arrive or leave, the first instructions to your little ones are probably "Give Grandma and Grandpa kisses," "Hug Auntie," and so on. Then, if as parents you hold hands, hug, and kiss in front of the children and smile at one another as you do so, you are reinforcing the idea that loving and touching are wonderful and natural. Watching you, your little ones learn that touching and kissing are all part of the process of loving and that, just as it's pleasant to receive, so it's important to give. Loving, they learn, is something everybody loves. At least the people they hug and kiss love it and encourage it. "Oh, that's my darling child. I love you," says any parent or grandparent lucky enough to get some sticky kisses and hugs.

Look at all the sexual information a three-year-old has acquired. She knows whether she's a girl. She knows it's better to be hugged than to be hurt, and that if she hugs and kisses, the people she is hugging and kissing like it. By the age of three, our toddlers have learned a lot about loving. If we are cold and withdrawn with one another and even with our children, we have provided them with another kind of sexual information without even saying a word about it. Babies and young children learn by experience and observation, not just by being told.

Kelly's parents were pleasant and affectionate with her but very reserved with each other when she was around. Their smiles were for her, not for each other. Kelly was a pleasant little girl, very obedient and well behaved, but shy and hard to get to know. She didn't seem to have the sense of fun that others in her play group did. She needed lots of reassurance and help. She almost looked troubled when a new game or new experience was suggested, almost as if there was something wrong somewhere but she couldn't figure out what. Kelly had learned another kind of sex/love information. She, too, had learned it by experience and observation. There were two ways of loving in her house: one for her, one for her parents.

Then there's another kind of sexual information that begins at the moment of birth—the information that the baby provides. Babies are born with a sex drive, a drive not so well developed as the drives to eat and to sleep, but a drive that is observable nonetheless. We know, for example, that baby boys can have erections at birth or shortly thereafter. We know that babies can masturbate before the age of three. We know that babies realize instinctively that touching a penis or clitoris is pleasurable in a way that touching an elbow or knee is not. As a matter of fact, it is not at all unusual for little boys, age one and up, to clutch their scrotums for pleasure and for reassurance. From birth, then, babies tell us that they know something about their bodies that they enjoy very much indeed.

Some parents get pretty upset when they find their little ones clutching their genitals in public. And, of course, it is rather disconcerting when, for example, you've dressed the children for a group portrait to find your little one ready to be recorded for posterity with his little hand firmly clutching his scrotum! What to do? In general, distract and/or substitute rather than make a fuss. Substitute a favorite toy to hold. Suggest building a tower with blocks. Taking that kind of action, distracting and/or substituting, makes this period more comfortable for parents. Later, you may want to let him know that this behavior is OK, but should be a private act. Remember: The *adults* have the problem. The kids are fine. And the more matter of fact and nonchalant we as parents can be, the better for everyone.

Teaching the Names of Body Parts

As we have seen, we teach our children a lot about sex and loving consciously and unconsciously—when we name their sex, for example, and when we model our own attitudes about loving. And babies teach us what they know instinctively about what feels good in terms of sex and love. It's a mutual process.

However, as parents you must also provide specific information about sex to your children at all ages as part of their education. Certainly children love to learn. They are curious about everything and delighted to have information. One of the first kinds of sexual information you can provide is teaching your toddler the names of her body parts. At the same age that you begin identifying and teaching the names of eyes and ears and legs and arms, you can incorporate nipples, penis, testicle, vagina, and anus. Note: We suggest using technical terms. Just as you wouldn't dream of finding a substitute for a neck or a nose, why would you substitute another name for a nipple? All parts of the body are miraculous and your child should enjoy knowing that. She should be able to take pride in every bit of her body and use it wisely and well. Boys are at a great advantage here—they can see their penis and testicles. Girls have a harder time with vagina, as there is little they can actually see. They do, however, learn that the area between their legs has a name.

Little children, two and under, are satisfied with names. As children become more verbal, they like to know what these organs do. And just as you say eyes are for seeing and ears are for hearing, so you would say penises are for urine and helping make babies, nipples are for milk, and anuses are for bowel movements. By approximately four years most children should know these organs and their function.

A nursing mother has a wonderful opportunity to demonstrate and explain the function of breast and nipple and milk to her young one. Usually a child tries to nurse her dolly. That's normal and appropriate. That's the way children work out what is going on. Their interest will last for a while; then the children will move on to something else. For example, the five-year-olds in our neighborhood had a teacher with enormous breasts. For a few weeks after school started, the group would stuff pillows under their shirts as they pretended to be Ms. B. Some even began comparing, saying "Mom, why aren't you as big as Ms. B?" Shortly, that intense interest turned elsewhere.

As any parent knows, information has to be repeated with little children. Once is never enough. Remember how you drilled your toddler about locating his nose, eyes, and ears? The same is true about teaching sexual parts of the body. Bath time is a natural time to reinforce this memory of parts of the body. You can say something like "What a big fine body you're growing. Your arms are growing—show me your arms. Your fingers are getting longer—show me your fingers. Your eyes don't get bigger but they see a lot—where are your eyes? Your ears hear a lot—where are your ears? Your hair is growing—show me your hair. Show me your penis. Show me your nipples. How about your elbow? Do you still have it? Where is it?" In other words, you can make a game of naming parts of the body, including sexual organs so that it is all very natural and easy.

Sometimes parents feel they should be undressed in front of their children, feeling that their nakedness helps the children feel more comfortable. Fine. If as parents you can be comfortable, that's excellent. Be prepared for a toddler to point or pull at a penis or breast and demand to know why his or hers is not as big or to ask why he or she has no hair. The downside risk for parents is that children may talk about these discoveries in what are, for you, inappropriate places. "Gosh, Grandpa—you should see Mommy's breasts. They're really big. How come boys don't have big breasts?" Or, "Grandma, Daddy has a big penis but I don't—mine is small."

If grandma and grandpa are uncomfortable you might say something like, "Isn't it wonderful, Grandma and Grandapa, how observant the children are. We are so proud that they know the names of their body parts. We hope you will be as proud as we are."

The variations on the theme are many and delightful and funny and okay. It's all part of your child's observing and learning and growing. Just be prepared to help Grandma and Grandpa with this information. They may need it. Your child is doing fine. She is observing, comparing, and drawing conclusions—just what she should be doing.

If natural modesty prevents you from being comfortable in front of your child, that's okay. Better to be natural than uncomfortable. Your discomfort will also make a statement to your children about what you really feel. If you do feel uncomfortable being naked around your youngster and she walks in on you, it might be helpful to talk about how you feel: "You know, everyone has a body and all women are built alike, as are all men. Some people don't mind having others see their bodies, but I do. This doesn't make me right or wrong, it just means I'm not comfortable having others see me with no clothes. So please knock before you come in. Okay?"

Remember, it is natural for children around the age of seven to become modest, regardless of their environment, and to insist that they can take their own baths, thank you, and that they need privacy also. We remember with delight Sarah, a five-year-old, who came to our house to enjoy a swim with Bets, a four-year-old. Bets was wearing a pair of trunks, Sarah a bathing suit that covered her chest. She looked at Bets with strong disapproval and said firmly, "At our age we should cover our breasts." Poor Bets didn't know what Sarah was talking about, but two years later she would insist on more formal and modest bathing attire without any prompting from Sarah.

We have been deliberately rather unspecific about when children should master body parts. Children verbalize at different ages. Some little ones are regular conversationalists at the age of two. Others are still babbling at that age. So it would be absurd to suggest that all three-year-olds, for example, know everything about the body. But by five, we would expect a child to know about her body and its functions . . . eyes are for seeing, ears are for hearing, the anus is for bowel movements, breasts are for milk, the mouth is for speech, and so on. Internal organs, such as liver and lungs, can wait.

Early Teaching About Sexual Abuse

Along with this information goes other information, which is much less fun to talk about but as important to provide. What we refer to, of course, is teaching your child about inappropriate or bad touching. Child abuse is not an issue exclusive to the seventies, eighties, and nineties. Given the number of adults, females in particular, who report having been sexually abused as children, it's tragic that parents didn't talk to their children about this generations ago. It is tough for some parents to face up to this. They'll say, "We've warned our children about getting into cars with strangers or accepting candy from strangers. That should do it." Well, maybe it should, but it doesn't. Ninety percent of all molesters are known to our children—and trusted. That includes neighbors, family friends, their older children, stepparents, grandparents and parents, teachers, clergy, doctors—the list goes on. Now, how do we warn our kids about people they know and trust and still expect those kids to be warm, happy, trusting individuals? It seems like a contradiction in terms. But it can and must be done. Remember, a molested child is never a happy child.

You have already taught your child about breasts, vaginas, penises, testicles, and anuses. You can refer to these organs as private parts—the parts that shorts or bathing suits cover. And just as you matter-of-factly warn your children about looking both ways before crossing a street, so you must warn your children about protecting themselves. Ideally, both parents are present when you have this talk, but either parent is effective. There are three points you want to make to your child:

1. *No one* has as a right to touch *your* private parts.

2. *No one* has a right to make *you* touch *their* private parts.

3. Being asked to touch another's private parts or having someone touch yours is *not* a secret you can keep. You must tell Mommy or Daddy if that happens, even if you've promised not to tell or even if you're told something awful will happen to you if you do tell. You must tell. It's true you should keep secrets, but this is a bad secret that you must *not* keep.

By the time your child is four, she should know these rules. Let's illustrate what we mean with a sample speech to use with a four-year-old girl. We would use bath time as a natural time for this kind of conversation.

"My goodness! What a fine body you've got. And you're growing so nicely. Pretty soon you will be a big girl. I'm very proud of your body and will help you take good care of it. We keep it clean with baths. We help it grow by giving you food. We make time for you to sleep and to play so that you'll be a fine, strong girl. We really have to take care of our bodies so that they will be healthy and strong like Daddy's and Mommy's. You know, when you fall down and hurt yourself, you come and tell us and if you're bleeding, we put on a Band-Aid. We do what we can to help you feel better because we love you and always will. And we always want you to tell us if something is wrong.

"Now, sometimes someone may want to touch your private parts—you know, the parts that your panties cover—your vagina and anus. Well, those are your private parts and even if you know and love the person who wants to touch you there, you say NO and come and tell Mommy and Daddy.

You just say, "NO! I can't do that." Then run and tell us. Sometimes someone you may even know and love, or someone you've never seen, may want you to touch his or her private parts, the parts that the bathing suit covers. Again, just say, "No, I can't do that." Then run and tell Mommy and Daddy. Just as we wouldn't let anyone hit you, we don't want anyone to touch your private parts either. And we don't want you to have to touch theirs.

"Now sometimes someone who wants to touch your private parts will tell you it's a secret and not to tell. Well, that's a bad secret and you have to tell Mommy and Daddy. You must never keep a bad secret from us. Ever. Anything that makes you feel funny—you just tell us about it. Even if the person says something awful will happen—to you or to us—if you tell, tell us anyway. We'll take care of it. Even if the person promises you a treat if you don't tell, tell us anyway. We love you and always want to help you to be safe."

What kind of tone should you use when you are having this talk with your child? Be loving and natural and serious as you say this. Just as you would warn your child against running across a street without looking both ways, or warn her about touching something fragile, so you warn her about this kind of danger.

If you're worried that your child will become paranoid or terrified of everybody, remember: You warned your child not to cross a street without looking. Do you know of any child who is afraid of cars as a result? Of course not. This is just another part of parenting that we have to do.

And boys need this information as well as girls; boys as well as girls are molested. It is imperative that we protect our sons as well as our daughters.

As we've said before and will say again, children learn by repetition. Just as you repeat warnings about safety, don't hesitate to repeat this one.

"Remember when we told you never to let anyone touch your private parts or ask you to touch theirs? Remember what we said to do? Yup. That's right."

Or you could incorporate the instructions into part of a general drill.

"What is our telephone number?"
"What is your name?"
"What is Daddy's name?"
"Where do you live?"
"What do you do if someone tries to touch your private parts or asks you to touch theirs?

Children are wonderful. They deserve to live a life that is as happy as we can make it. Keeping them informed and safe is one way to provide a happy childhood.

Just as you feel comfortable talking to your little ones about body parts and just as you feel comfortable hugging and kissing, so you can be comfortable answering your children's questions about their bodies and about what you have told them. And children do have questions.

For example, three-year-olds are fascinated with the whole process of urinating and bowel movements. They have just lately mastered the art of toilet training and are very proud of it. Now girls find that they sit down to urinate and boys don't. Girls want to know why. Actually, the answer is very practical: If they tried standing up to urinate, they'd get urine running down their legs. Little boys, on the other hand, adore urinating just about anywhere with their newly mastered penises.

One mother was pretty startled when a neighbor complained that her little boy was urinating in the bushes. When she asked her son why he wasn't coming in to use the toilet, he looked at her, smiled, and said joyously, "But it's much more fun to use the bushes. I love it."

Carrie, a three-year-old girl, astonished her mother who had taken her into a public toilet. "So long, bowel movements," she shouted suddenly as the water began to swirl. "Good-bye." Her mother, a little red-faced, said, "She's never done that before. I don't know what people thought." We hope that those who heard were amused.

This age group considers bathroom humor hilarious. They enjoy discussing all aspects with their friends and family. Although we have been using formal terms like "urine" and "bowel movement," children quickly learn that "pee" and "poo-poo" and other such terms are easier to use. That's okay, unless they learn the four-letter words for such functions. It's okay to object to their using that kind of language, if that is the way you feel. But there is nothing wrong with their learning more formal usage either. Although it seems as if they will never get interested in anything else, it really *is* a stage that will pass. Don't make a big deal of it. Think of it this way: They've earned the right. It really is a big accomplishment to learn to use a toilet like Mom and Dad.

Children want to know why they have to wash their hands after a bowel movement. Again, there's a practical answer— germs. That's why we don't urinate in bath water or anywhere else but in a toilet, which washes the germs away. Simple answers satisfy children of this age. "Why don't I have a penis?" little girls want to know. "Why don't girls have a penis?" little boys want to know. They're happy to learn that that is the difference between little boys and girls. Girls don't have penises and boys do. Well, how do girls urinate, then? They have a special place between their legs for that and it works very well. Just be prepared to have all this explained to some friend or relative at some (for you), inappropriate time.

Early Teaching On Where Babies Come From

Four-year-olds are more interested than younger children in how babies are made. It's very puzzling for them to hear that Daddy plants a special seed called a sperm into a special place in Mommy. Mommy has an egg, and if the sperm and egg meet, a baby comes. It doesn't clarify things for them to learn that only girls can have babies and only boys can plant sperm because they have a penis. Often children want to know if Mommy and Daddy do that. Then the next question often is, "Can I watch?" That question provides a splendid opportunity to explain that it's something grownups do when they love each other very much—and that it's also something mothers and fathers do privately.

If by chance your child wanders in when you are making love, quietly explain that this is a private time and that you need to be alone. You will play with them later. You need only act relaxed.

One mother was pretty startled when her four-year-old wanted to know how not to have babies. Mom was temporarily stumped. Then she remembered to keep it simple. "Well, if Moms and Dads don't get together, then they don't make babies." Her child was satisfied with that.

Five-year-olds often want to know why there aren't more babies in the house. This is a time to explain that it takes time to make a baby. You can remind them how hard it was for them to learn to ride a bike, and assure them that it's kind of like that.

Sex play between children starts about this time. It's natural. Just as the kindergarten children we described earlier put pillows under their shirts to try to have a bosom like Ms. B, so children experiment, trying to make sense out of what they have heard. That's the way children create order for themselves: They act it out. It is disconcerting for most parents, however, when they find a five-year-old boy examining their five-year-old girl's chest. It's natural for the children, but hard for the parents. The best thing is to keep your cool. Try distracting and substituting. For example:

"Who'd like some milk and cookies?"
"Who'd like to hear a new story?"
"Let's see who can jump the highest."

Please note: We are not sanctioning a thirteen-year-old investigating a five-year-old. That's another matter altogether and one that you would want your child to report.

When a new baby arrives, the older child often wants to know if he can taste Mommy's milk also. This is a time to laugh and hug and say, "You can eat steak and ice cream and candy. All this baby can eat is milk so we have to save it for him. Just the way I did when you were a baby. You were the only one to get this special milk. But how would you like a cookie? That's something the baby can't have."

It's fascinating to watch these little minds grow. It's fascinating to hear how they figure things out. If we smile and encourage their questions and observations when they are young, it makes it much easier to continue our dialogue about love and sex as they mature. We are laying the groundwork for trust and intimacy as we do so.

CHAPTER THREE

How We Continue:
From Six To Eight Years

The ages from six to eight provide a kind of breathing space for parents. If we look backward to the amount of growth our children made from infancy to five years of age, we find it staggering. In five short years, our children have learned to feed and dress themselves, sleep through the night, master toilet training, walk, talk, and accumulate a sizeable vocabulary. They have even achieved a certain amount of independence; generally they are willing to spend time with a grandparent or sitter without feeling utterly abandoned.

New Authority Figures

In their hurry to learn, children ask innumerable questions. Just about everything in the world is fascinating and amazing. Why is the sky blue? How come I have only two ears? Why does Jimmy have brown eyes and I don't? Are there enough chairs in heaven for all the people who are up there? It goes on and on. And all of it is just as it should be. It's a pity that we lose that sense of wonder and excitement as we get older.

As children move on to school, however, they lose the rapid growth patterns of early childhood. They don't have the dramatic mastery of skills, as do infants and toddlers. There is much less celebration of new skills. No more talk of, "He rolled over today." "He said 'Mama.' " "He took his first step alone." School is exciting, but the mastery of skills occurs over a period of time. Our children, however brilliant, don't learn to read overnight so that we can report the achievement to proud grandparents and friends. The quiet mastery of school skills now is accompanied by a growing awareness of new authorities. For preschool children, the ultimate authorities are Mommy and Daddy. "It is *so* true. My Mommy said so." "It does *too* go like that. My Daddy said so." But when our children start school, new authorities appear.

Teachers, for example, seem to know as much as Mommy and Daddy. And maybe they know even more. And friends become increasingly important and knowledgeable. If our children have older siblings, those siblings often become authorities also, particularly in the areas of dress and manners. As parents, we begin to hear more of "Susan's mother lets her wear nylons. Why can't I?" Or, "How come Alice can stay up later than I can?" "How come Steve can watch more TV than I can? It's not fair!" Instead of being content with what is, our children are now beginning to watch, compare, and criticize. Values become more important than facts: Getting enough sleep is less important than the right to do what others are doing.

By now, parental authority begins to crumble. Friends are becoming just as important and maybe even more authoritative. This is the beginning of the refrain, "Yeah, but Charlie says so." This is to be expected. As we encourage our children to have more independence and visit with their friends after school, they expand their sources of information. For example, you may be very careful about what TV you allow your children to see, or what magazines you allow your children to look at, but that doesn't mean that the neighbors agree or are as watchful. Therefore, your children may now be exposed to more explicit TV shows or movies than you would allow.

Children are also exposed to whatever information their friends and their friends' older siblings may provide. This is all part of the growing-up process. There's little you can do to prevent "premature" learning of this sort short of insisting that children stay at home with you—and that kind of isolation is as bad as having your children become more precocious than you might wish. So as parents, what you can do is to help your children establish sound values and provide them with accurate information—*and* let them know that you are there for them whenever they have a question. You are the ones who want to help them get the right information.

Reinforcing Important Values

Suppose you find your six-year-old daughter experimenting with makeup and trying to be more grown up than you wish. Remember that if you make a big deal of this, saying something on the order of, "Oh, what are you doing? Go wash your face. Don't ever let me see you looking like that again," your little girl will know that something is going on and will want to try it again, only this time more secretly. It's more effective to laugh and say, "Well, who is this painted daisy? It's fun to dress up and pretend, but remember that it is pretend. And it's just something to do when you are pretending to be grown up. How about wearing it now and washing it off before dinner?" Or, if your little boy is suddenly bragging about how he likes to catch girls and kiss them, it is better to say quietly, "Do the girls like that? If they don't like it, do you really want to make people unhappy? Do you think they will like you if you make them unhappy? We think it's nice to have people like us. We think it's kind of mean to make people unhappy. Why don't we see if we can find things you can do to give you pleasure and still make people happy and then like you?" In other words, you can help your children establish appropriate values by encouraging rather than scolding.

The same kind of calm is what you want when you begin to address the more explicit kinds of sexual questions they will start asking.

Answering Questions

Because children are more preoccupied with friendships and groups like Little League and Brownies doesn't mean they've lost interest in their bodies and bodily functions; TV and their friends will see to that. So you have to continue providing your children with the kind of information they request. Although you may answer all their questions before they started school, they still need to ask, and to ask, and to ask.

There's a line from *Bye Bye, Birdie*, a musical from the fifties, where one of the parents comments that he didn't know what puberty was until he was past it. Ah, the good old days. They're gone, we fear, along with the dinosaurs. Children are more precocious and so are their bodies. Girls are menstruating earlier, and the number of teenage pregnancies in this country makes its own statement. So children can't wait until puberty has passed. We *must* continue to educate and guide them.

The questions that continue to perplex children center around the following subjects:

How are babies made?

Why do I have a penis?

Why don't I have a penis?

Do you make a baby every time?

Do you do that?

Do you have to be married to make a baby?

Can I watch you try?

You notice that these questions aren't a lot different from the kinds of questions your children asked when they were younger. What is different is that now the answers are fuller, for children can understand more and even compare information with friends. It still doesn't matter who does the explaining, Mom or Dad. Ideally, parents could explain together, but in real life, at the time your child asks for information, one parent or the other is away. We think it's best to answer your child promptly rather than say, "Wait till your father (or mother) gets back. Then we will talk to you." Postponement makes a big deal out of a natural occurrence, and who wants to delay immediate gratification in this area? We certainly don't!

Suppose your child wants to know what "pregnant" means. You could say:

> "Oh, I'm glad you asked me that. Pregnant means that a woman is going to have a baby. Did you know that it takes nine months for the baby to grow big enough to be born? That means that a woman is pregnant for nine months while she is waiting for her baby to be born. During those nine months her tummy will get bigger so that the baby will have enough room to grow. At the end of nine months, the baby will be born and then the woman will not be pregnant any longer. You know, Tom's mother is pregnant. We'll watch her and see how her tummy gets bigger and bigger."

At that point, your child may lose interest and walk away. Or, your child may ask again how the baby got in the tummy in the first place. You thought you had explained it all to him when he was three, and here we go again! But this time, provide more information. You could continue with something like this:

> "Well, that's just the right question, but it's a kind of long answer so listen carefully. Please ask questions if I say something you don't understand. In order to make a baby, two things have to happen: A man's seed has to meet a woman's egg and fertilize it. That's true for most animals—an egg has

to be fertilized by a male's seed in order for another animal to appear. You know that hens lay eggs. But if the eggs aren't fertilized by a rooster's seed, then no new chickens appear. A rooster is a male, you see, and a hen is a female. Well, the same thing is true for mothers and daddies. Men make seeds or semen in their testicles. Women make seeds in their ovaries. When a man places his penis in a woman's vagina, he leaves seeds or sperm there. If a woman's egg has traveled down to the vagina at the same time, and her egg is fertilized by his sperm, then a baby is started. It's all pretty marvelous. Does it make sense to you?"

Again, your child may be satisfied, distracted, or bored at this point. If not, you may expect further questions and answers:

"Well, what's a vagina?"

"Good question. That's a special place that women have inside their bodies, sort of below their belly buttons. You can't see it. It's not like a penis. It's inside. But it is a special place for egg and sperm to meet. And that's where men put their penises, in a very special loving way."

"Does it hurt?"

"No, if a man puts his penis there in a very loving way and that is what a woman wants him to do, then it doesn't hurt at all. It is a very loving act."

"Well, how does the egg get to the vagina?"

"Oh, you do ask the right questions. Women have ovaries that are placed above the vagina. The ovaries make one egg a month. When the egg is ready, it leaves the ovaries and travels down a tube to the vagina. As I said, if the egg meets a sperm and is fertilized, then a baby is started."

"What if a woman forgets to make an egg?"

"Fortunately, women don't even have to think about it. The body does it automatically. You know, you breathe every day, every minute, but you don't have to think about it, you just do it. It's sort of like that. It's kind of like making urine. The body does it. You don't do anything about it. You just have to go to the bathroom a few times a day and get rid of it."

"Does Daddy put his penis in your vagina?"

"Yes, he does."

"Then how come we don't have more babies? How come I'm the only one around here?"

"Well, there isn't always an egg waiting. Remember, the egg comes just once a month and it's hard to know when exactly that will be."

"What happens if the egg comes and there's no sperm?"

"Good question. The egg, if it doesn't get fertilized by a sperm, just flows out of the body."

"Does that hurt?"

"Nope. No more than it hurts when you urinate."

"Oh, good. But what if Dad's urine comes when he puts his penis in your vagina? That would be yucky."

"Yes, it would be yucky but it never happens because there is a little valve that turns off the urine that can come when a penis is in the vagina. Naturally, when the penis comes out of the vagina, the valve turns again so that a man can urinate if he has to."

"Do you have to be married to put a penis in a vagina?"

"No, you don't. But it's much better if you are married because, if a baby is made, then it is much better for the baby to have both a mother and a father, just the way that you do."

"Well, listen, when the baby comes out, how does it get out?"

"Through the vagina, through a special opening that all women have. It is separate from where urine comes from."

"When can I do that?"

"When you're grown up and married."

"Well, if I'm good, can I watch you and Dad? Then I can learn how to do it."

"No, it's a private time. No one can watch. It's also a very loving time. I guess that's why we love you so much."

"Well, how will I learn how to do it?"

"When the time comes, we'll tell you all about it so that you will know everything you will need to know."

Don't be surprised if your child asks some pretty frank questions:

"Does Grandpa put his penis in Grandma?"

"Yes. Everyone who has had a baby has done that."

"What if I don't?"

"Well, then, you won't have a baby."

"Hey, listen, I'd better tell Alice all about this. I'll be back later."

"Maybe you ought to let her parents tell her. They like to be the ones to do it. But you and I can talk about it any time.'

"Does Dad know all this stuff?"

"Indeed he does, and he'll talk to you about it, too, any time you want. I wish he'd been here with me but he is at the office. He'll be sorry he missed it."

"Maybe he doesn't know. Maybe I'd better tell him."

"Well, that might be a good idea. Then if you have other questions, you can ask him."

"Okay. When are we having dinner?"

As we have pointed out before, rarely do these conversations occur at an ideal time so that you're cool and prepared. Caught off-guard, you may find yourself flustered or embarrased. If so, it's best to acknowledge that:

"Good question. I was looking forward to talking to you again about these things, but I guess I just wasn't thinking about it just now so I'm a little flustered. I've got to get my head on straight. You know, no one ever answered my questions when I was little, so I'm not quite sure how to go about it. But I always want to answer your questions about anything whenever I can, so fire away and I'll do the best I can."

Just remember, you're a parent, not an encyclopedia. If you don't know the answer, say so. What a splendid model you provide if you say, "No, I don't know the name of the opening where the girl's urine comes out, but we'll look it up and find out. Isn't it a good thing we both know how to read!"

Furthermore, if you're proud of the way you're handling this, be sure to pat yourself on the back. You deserve it. Rarely does a child congratulate you or thank you. When he's had enough, he's on to the next thing. Incidentally, respect your child's need to change the subject. Children don't have the attention span we do. When they've had enough, they lose interest totally. When they're ready for more, they'll come back. You have already demonstrated that you're ready and willing to talk to them at any time. Because you have proven it, your child will trust you and return.

Becoming A Good Listener

We have talked a lot about the trust that you want your children to have in you. You want them to feel they can turn to you in perfect confidence that you will do what you can for them without question. But, in addition to having information for them and conveying this information, there is yet another task that you have to perform in order to demonstrate that you are really trustworthy. You have to be respectful of their confidences. That's somewhat different from the way you treated what they said at three or four. Remember the pleasure you took in telling your friends and relatives the cute thing Bobby said? "Bobby wants to know if his penis will fall off when he grows up and then will he be a girl?" It didn't matter if Bobby were standing beside you while you recounted the latest. You would probably smile and hug him as you told the story and let him know how adorable he was to ask such a question but, by the time Bobby is six, he doesn't care to have his confidences advertised. Be careful. Now is the time to model good listening. Here are the rules.

- *Don't betray confidences.* If your daughter overhears you telling Grandmother how she asked the following question—ha, ha, ha—her feelings will be hurt. It may be a long time before she trusts you again.

- *Try to be natural.* You wouldn't get flustered if your child asked why it rained. If he asks why he has a penis, tell him, "You're a boy. All boys have penises. Even boy dogs, boy cats, etc. That's how we know who is a boy and who isn't."

- *Don't interrupt and don't be impatient.* Don't try to put words in your child's mouth. Don't urge him to hurry up and finish what he is saying. He'll work it out. If you have run out of time, then make an appointment with your youngster so that he can finish later. "Oh, dear. I love talking with you but I have to get the baby to the doctor's, and I don't have time to talk to you now. But I know what we're talking about is important. Can we continue after dinner tonight? Right after the baby goes to bed?" Then make sure that you do.

- *Be encouraging.* "Say, that sounds like an important question. I'm glad you asked me that. That's just the right thing to do. Good for you."

- *Don't put your child down.* "You don't know that? How come? I thought everyone knew that. What's the matter with you anyhow?"

- *Don't get angry with your child if he uses language that is offensive to you.* He's trying to ask you something that is important to him and he may be using the language that he heard that he needs to know about. You have talked about urine and penises. He may suddenly refer to piss and wee-wees. It's more helpful to acknowledge his expanding vocabulary but then caution him about where and when it's appropriate to use it. For example, if he wants to know if Dads piss when they put their penis or wee-wee in a vagina, answer the question before tackling the language. "Of course, when you're with your friends, you're going to use the words they use. But when you're with me or other grown-ups, please use the words I've taught you. It's much more respectful." We remember with amusement an angelic-looking six-year-old boy laughing happily one night, and explaining there wasn't a single dirty word he didn't know or use. There was no point in telling him never to use those words. His pride in possessing them was too strong. But his parents could and did caution him about where he could get in trouble using street language.

• *If your child asks a question at an inappropriate time, tell him you'll be glad to get back to the question, and then be sure that you do.* For example, if your child points at a woman in a crowd and says loudly, "How come she's got a big tummy?" it's okay to say firmly, "I'll tell you all about it when we get home. Right now, we don't want to make the lady feel uncomfortable." This way, you kill two birds with one stone: in this case, pregnancy and good manners. (You are teaching, "We never want to make anyone feel uncomfortable. Yet we still respect your questions.")

Now you may find yourselves armed with all kinds of information and excellent resolutions about being good listeners, but no one is asking questions! But that doesn't mean your child doesn't have them. He just isn't asking, for some reason or other. It's all right to decide to start a discussion yourself rather than waiting for him to come to you. But do it in a natural sort of way. Perhaps you and your child have to go somewhere in the car. That's a good way to use the time, when you're not pressed for time and you're both together in a rather private area. "Say, did you know that Tom's mother just had a baby? Had you known that she was pregnant? Listen. Do you know what I mean by pregnant? Do you remember what I told you about how babies are born?" And so on.

Incidentally, it is still important for children at this age to be reminded about good and bad touching, private parts of the body, and telling responsible adults. Unluckily, premenstrual girls are particularly appealing to molesters because they don't get pregnant. We can't count the number of women who have told us that their agonies of sexual abuse began at the age of seven or eight and continued until they menstruated.

You can continue reminding your child about this in the form of a quiz:

"What's the thing to do if someone wants to touch your private parts or have you touch his?"

"What if it's someone you know and like?"

"Whom will you tell?"

"What would you do if a stranger, or even someone you knew and liked, offered to give you a puppy or a treat if you went with him?"

"What if someone threatened to hurt us if you didn't go with him?"

Please remember that although your child has been warned and reminded, if something does happen, it is NEVER your child's fault. It is always the older person's fault. It is imperative that children retain their self-respect. If your child fell down a flight of stairs, would you scold him for being klutzy, or would you rush to comfort him? The same is true in incest or sexual assault cases. You must teach your child that he is okay. Somebody else was bad, but the child was not. This distinction is vital because otherwise the child feels a sense of guilt, thinks he deserves to be victimized, and then loses his self-respect. In addition, be aware that a child who sees himself a victim then acts as a victim throughout his life. No child deserves that.

By being warm and accepting and respectful, you model trust and intimacy for your children. You have encouraged them to confide in you. What better preparation can there be as you prepare them and yourselves for the next stage?

CHAPTER FOUR

What Preteens Need to Know: From Nine to Twelve Years

This is the beginning of the "fasten your seat belt" time. We are getting ready for more dramatic changes with our children. Changes have been gradual for the past few years, but now young bodies start to accelerate in growth. These are the active, developing years, which forecast the adolescence that is to follow. As all parents know or have correctly guessed, the adolescent years are easily the most important ones of a child's sexual development, and usually the hardest for parents. Therefore, coaching parents about the preteen period is like preparing the team for the season before the big game.

Teaching About Bodily Changes

In order to simplify that coaching, and keep the focus of this book on you, the parents, and how you can present sexual information to your children so that they will turn out to be healthy, loving kids, we have made you a chart. It probably is not "everything you have to know about puberty and were afraid to ask," but it *is* complete enough to do the job. It is easy to follow and you can refer back to it whenever you get frazzled and need to get your facts straight.

In the chart, we have separated information about boys

and girls for obvious reasons: They not only have different sexual development, they develop at different ages. We have also separated their development into four categories that we hope will be helpful as you talk and interact with your children.

The four categories are:

- *General physical development.* This includes all body development except the sexual organs.

- *Sexual physical development.* This includes sexual organs and secondary sexual organs (like pubic hair).

- *Emotional development.* These are changes in *feeling*.

- *Social Development.* This involves interactions mostly with peers but also with adults.

We have made a second chart, this one for the kids. It is a much simplified and shorter version of the first one. It is designed to do two things: summarize for you the information we think your preteen should know, and provide information boys and girls should know about themselves *and* each other. Boys need to know what is happening to girls, and girls do much better understanding and managing male sexuality if they also know about boys.

You may show the second chart to your children if you wish. It eliminates worrisome terms like anxiety and defensiveness—things you may not wish to share with your child at this stage. You may, of course, feel that you *do* want to discuss things in the larger chart. Some kids do better knowing and talking about pretty mature material. The choice is yours; stay loose and trust your judgment about your own child.

INFORMATION FOR PARENTS
Boys: Ages Nine to Twelve

General Physical Development

Taller
Broader
More muscles
Greater strength
Breast swelling and tenderness
More perspiration; Body odor

Oilier hair and skin
Hairier arms and legs
Underarm hair
Beard develops
Pimples; Possible acne
Voice change

Sexual Physical Development

Sexual fantasies
More erections
Pubic hair: starts straight, grows kinkier
Growing penis
Growing scrotum

Wrinklier scrotum
Looser scrotum
Baggier scrotum
Ejaculation
Nocturnal emissions
Masturbation increases

Emotional Development

Stronger sexual feelings
Sensitive to failures, mistakes, and fears
Anxiety about sexual fantasies and masturbation
Stronger interest in girls, yet attempts to hide it

Sexual interest in girls
Self-image shaky
Struggle to gain control of self, be manly
Perceptual distortion
Defensiveness

Social Development

Interest in other sex
Struggle for social skills: dancing, parties, conversation
Appear manly socially: identify with social male stereotypes (macho, strong-silent, protective, etc.)
Overreaction to failures and mistakes in peer relations
Face heavy demands for achievement in some special field that he can identify as "his"—like fixing cars, climbing, bicycling, etc.

Growing interest in television and video cassette recordings: adventure, sports, commercialization of sex in advertisements, drama
Face heavy demand for scholastic achievement, especially in competition with girls
Avoid closeness—including modesty and avoidance of touching and nudity
Secret clubs or gangs

INFORMATION FOR PARENTS
Girls: Ages Nine to Twelve

General Physical Development

Earlier growth spurts than boys, taller for about two years

Temporary weight gains: three to five pounds

Rounding and filling out of hips, buttocks, thighs, and shoulders

Breasts grow

Swelling and tenderness of breasts and extremities

Backache

Tenderness of abdomen, bloated

More perspiration; Body odor

Increasing body hair

Underarm hair

Possible fuzzy hair on lips

Pimples; Possible acne

Change in vaginal discharge

Increased appetite or thirst

Alternation of extra energy and lack of energy

Menstruation

Sexual Physical Development

Sexual fantasies

Growing vulva

Fluids begin to appear in vulva area and vagina

Masturbation increases

Pubic hair: starts straight, grows kinkier

Clitoral stimulation more sexually arousing

Emotional Development

Stronger sexual feelings

Sensitive to failures, mistakes, and fears

Mood shifts

Tension; Anxiety

Interest in boys

Concentration varies: may increase and/or decrease

Irritability

Self-image shaky

Perceptual distortion

Defensiveness

Social Development

Avoid closeness, avoid nudity and touch

Bursts of social activity: dancing, parties, more interest in group activities

Appear womanly socially: identify with social sex stereotypes (seductive, mothering, etc.)

Intense reaction to failures, mistakes, and rejection in social peer relations

Higher scholastic achievement than boys

More interest and awareness of love stories and events like marriage and birth

Exposure to public sex: television, video cassettes, movies, advertisements, etc.

Interest in other sex

INFORMATION FOR BOYS AND GIRLS
Ages Nine to Twelve

Boys	Girls
Growth spurt	Growth spurt
Early voice changes	
Straight pubic hair	Straight pubic hair
Perspiration and body odor	Perspiration and body odor
Pimples and acne	Pimples and acne
Underarm hair	Underarm hair
Testes and penis begin growing	Breasts enlarge
Erections	
Kinky pubic hair	Kinky pubic hair
Marked voice changes	
Ejaculation becomes possible	Menstruation begins
Beard develops	
Nocturnal emissions	
Masturbation	Masturbation

Let's talk about the big chart and how we imagine you might use it. We'll try to re-create some of the talks we have had with children and their parents, and we will address some of the more difficult issues.

Since we believe it is helpful for kids to have some information about what is going to happen to their bodies and psyches in advance, many of our little dialogues take place with children before they reach preteen age.

Preparing for Bodily Changes

Let's start with Davy. He is nine years old and he is bright and observant. He likes to talk with his Dad, but his parents are divorced. Dad lives a good distance away and does not see Davy often enough to keep up with the questions Davy asks. It's Saturday, one of the days Dad should be there, but isn't. Maybe Dad's absence is what is really bothering Davy underneath his aggressive curiosity, but no matter—Mother is the parent on-site and she catches it—broadside. She has been working all week, and naturally she is a little tired. She doesn't allow herself to feel tired, though—she is one of those dedicated parents who would rather feel guilty than admit fatigue.

Davy: Mom, where are you?

Mother: Out here on the porch, dear.

Davy: [*Arriving on the porch*] What are you doing?

Mother: Just reading the paper, dear—you can see that—so I guess there is something you want.

Davy: No, Mom, just something funny happened and I was wondering about it.

Mother: What was it?

Davy: Well, you know Jimmy, well—he was trying to yell for the ball—Billy was on first—and his voice sort of went up and down and finally all he could get out was a squeak. We all laughed so hard that Billy just dropped the ball. It was really funny.

Mother: You all laughed? Did Jimmy mind? That wasn't very nice.

Davy: No, *Mother*, he didn't mind, he knew it sounded funny and he laughed, too.

Mother: Okay—I was just asking. You said you were wondering about it. Were you wondering why it happened?

Davy: Yes, I was, because Dad told me that boys' voices change and get deep like his, and that mine would some day. Do you know anything about that?

Mother: Well, I just might, you know. As a matter of fact, I know something you know, too, about Jimmy.

Davy: What's that?

Mother: He had a birthday last week—his twelfth— we were both there. You ate and I served, remember?

Davy: I remember, sure. Say, Mom, when will my voice change? Do you know? Dad didn't.

Mother: Nobody knows for sure, David, but within a couple of years something ought to happen. Did Dad mention any other things to you? Like getting more muscles and hair?

Davy: He said that if I exercise a lot I would be strong. But he didn't say anything about my hair growing.

Mother: Well, now that you brought it up, maybe I can tell you a few things that you can check with Dad when you see him, okay?

Davy: Sure, what things do you mean? About Jimmy?

Mother: Yes, you might say they are about any boy, and when you get as old as Jimmy you would want to know why your voice squeaked, too, wouldn't you?

Davy: Sure, Mom, you know me, I like to know everything!

Mother: Well, that's good, because some of the things I want to tell you are about your own body, and it might be a bit embarrassing.

Davy: I won't be embarrassed, *Mother.*

Mother: Well, Mother just might be, but we'll try it anyway. You see, when you get a little older, lots of things about your body are going to change. This happened to Jimmy, and it happened to Dad, and it happens to girls, too, in different ways.

Davy: In what different ways?

Mother: Let's talk about that after we talk about you and your body. Sure, you will get bigger—not only taller but suddenly you will notice that all those muscles you want start appearing almost by themselves.

Davy: Really?

Mother: Yes, it's almost magical and it's caused by certain things, called hormones, that your glands begin to supply to your growing body.

Davy: And is it those hormone things that caused Jimmy to squeak?

Mother: That's right, and it has caused or is going to cause him to have some other changes, too.

Davy: Like what?

Mother: Well, you remember that Dad told you what the word "genitals" means—and maybe you have noticed that when you have seen some of the older boys naked in the shower at gym—they are growing hair around their genitals?

Davy: Sure, just like Dad.

Mother: Right. Well, that is one of the things that will happen to you, along with growing hair under your arms, in the armpits, you know—

Davy: Yeah, I know *that*.

Mother: Sure you do. But did you know that hair will grow *on* your arms and legs, too?

Davy: But, Mom, won't all that hair under my arms and things feel awful?

Mother: Not really. It has a purpose, you see—it actually makes it easier because the skin doesn't rub against itself and cause irritation. And another thing hair goes along with is—hey, are you interested in this stuff, or do you want me to quit talking about it for now?

Davy: Well, finish what you are saying and then maybe you could make sausages for lunch?

Mother: Okay, it's a deal. I was saying that along with the hair goes an increase in perspiration; you will notice that you will sweat more. And that means you need to be more careful about baths and maybe even use a deodorant—you know, the stuff you put under your arms.

Davy: I used it already—Dad let me try it. It felt funny and didn't seem to do much.

Mother: Sure, that's because at your age you don't really need it. Was it the same brand as Dad's aftershave?

Davy: Yeah, same smell.

Mother: Well, that's where more hair is going to grow—right on your face and you will . . .

Davy: . . . have a beard, right?

Mother: Well, you will probably start with a few mustache hairs—but that's enough for now. Sausages?

Davy: You promised!

Mother: I know—and let's promise to continue at another time with what happens to your body as you grow older, okay? There is lots more to learn. And ask Dad about this, too. I'll tell him about our conversation today and maybe you two can continue with it. Now— sausages coming up!

Did you notice some of the nice moves Davy's mother made as she guided the conversation along? Right at the beginning she set the tone of consideration for others when dealing with sexual change by asking whether Jimmy had been hurt by the boys laughing at him. Then, when Davy mentioned Dad's participation in sexual education, Mother supported that and continued to enhance Dad's role right through, even suggesting that she would inform Dad of what she had started so that Dad might pick it up from there, if he wished.

Mother also made the decision to bypass Davy's request for information about girls. She wanted to keep the focus on Davy's own body for now, feeling that such focus would ease the way for her to tell him about girls later. After all, she is the expert on girls' bodies and can save that for a later time when Jimmy is grounded a bit by data on his own body. She is going to give Dad a chance to teach male body things to Davy. She knows that if Dad doesn't make it happen within a reasonable length of time, she can pick it up and do the job.

After all, she and her husband are separated. She recognizes that reality and also accepts the reality that personal experience in body sexual development has a value. Dad can tell Davy things about his *feelings* about the body changes he experienced that Mother would have difficulty expressing. Is Mother being sexist? Is she copping out? Should only Dad talk to the boys and only Mother talk to the girls? Probably not; this mother is making judgments not only

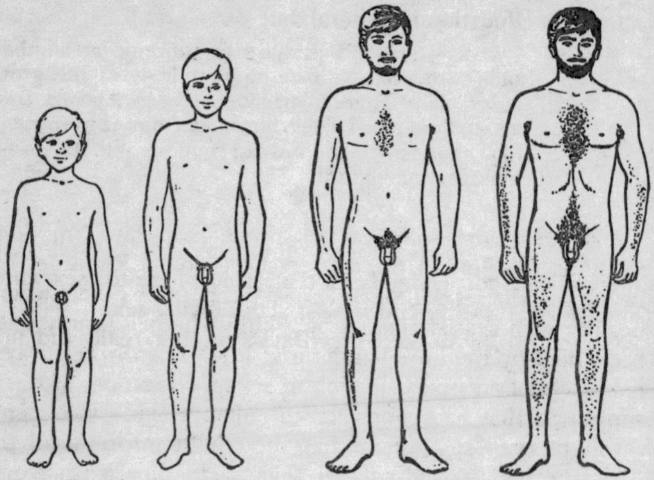

Development of Hair, Muscles, and Genitalia in Males

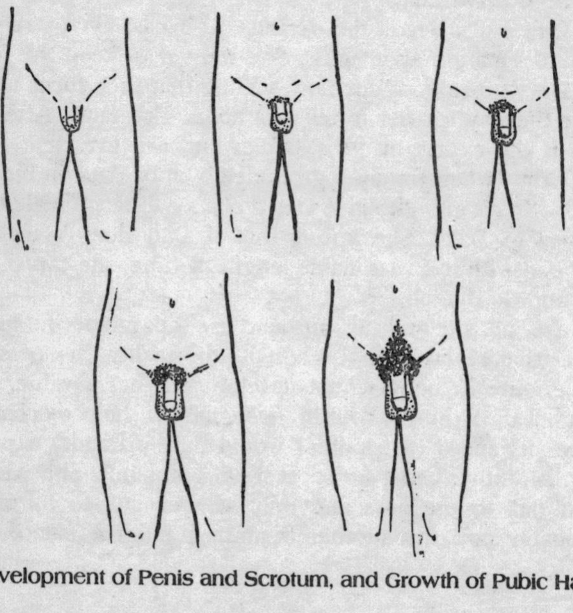

Development of Penis and Scrotum, and Growth of Pubic Hair

about sex education in general, but also about sex education *with* love. Most important of all, she is aware that as a divorced mother, her role in teaching sex requires extra tact and wisdom. She also seems to have made a judgment that, given a chance, Dad will come through. She is going to give Dad a shot at it because that will re-create for Davy the mutual support he might have had without the divorce. That support is loving support, and Mother wants all these sexual facts presented in an atmosphere of love, hoping there will be a transfer from that atmosphere to "sex-with-love" for Davy. She knows a lot about loving sex.

You probably noticed that Davy's mother really did not cover a great deal of information in her talk. Did you feel that she quit too soon? Maybe so, but we'd like to show you another illustration that goes a little further. We are still following the chart, and the next dialogue begins where Davy's mother left off.

Preparing for Puberty in an Intact Family

Let's set the scene. This time we have a married couple with a son just under ten years old—a bit older than Davy. The son, Jason, is the couple's second child. Their firstborn is Julie; she is thirteen. They have another little one, Claire, who has just turned three. Mom and Dad have been married sixteen years and things are good. They have worked hard and have earned what they have; they are well-informed and have read a lot. Since Jason is their second child, they have had some experience teaching Julie about sex, but that was different—AIDS and child abuse were not recognized as important factors then.

As we enter their home one evening to listen in on what Dad and Jason are saying, there is one more thing we have to know in order to understand what is going on. Mom and Dad had purchased some good books on teaching children about sex when they were bringing up Julie. Dad recently purchased a new one to help him and Mother do the same for Jason, and he had *deliberately* left it around where Jason might see it and pick it up. Since the family reads a lot, there was nothing unusual about books being left around, and Jason had taken the bait. He is reading it—in Dad's favorite chair, of course, in the little room that Dad uses as an office.

Dad comes in quietly, through the open door.

Dad: So you found our new book. That's good.

Jason: Is it "good"? Gee, Dad, maybe you don't want me to be looking at this. I just sort of picked it up when I came in looking for your calculator. I've got math homework to do over the weekend and . . .

Dad: No, I want you to look at that book. Frankly, that's why I left it out. I hoped you might find it and then we could talk about it. How about talking right now? Let's take some time.

Jason: Well—okay—if it's all right with you.

Dad: Just one thing: Let me get Mother. I want her to join us.

Jason: Gee, Dad, is this going to be one of those family talks or something? I didn't know it was so important.

Dad: It's not going to be a family talk, Jason—just you, Mother, and I. And yes, this is very important . . .

Jason: I wish I hadn't picked it up. I *knew* something would happen.

Dad: No, Jason, it's not important because you did something wrong. You did everything right. You are a normally curious kid and you picked up a book that we left around because we want you to understand what is going to happen to your body as you get older. That's what is important.

Jason: What's going to happen to my body? I'm going to get bigger, aren't I?

Dad: Sure you are. And your body will change in other ways as well. Mom and I will explain that—now, there she is. Hey, Nancy, can you join us for a talk?

Mother: Oh, you found the book, huh, Jason? What did you think of it?

Jason: I don't know. It says funny things—like, what is "perspiration," Mom?

Mother: Exactly the same thing as sweat—"perspiration" is just a bigger, sort of nicer-sounding word for it.

Jason: So what is so special about sweating and growing up?

Dad: What's special is that when you grow up your skin changes.

Jason: Yes, I remember. You said then that my skin would get oilier and I'd get pimples. Do I have to get pimples? Did you get pimples?

Dad: I got some, but they were not bad. I think that being on the basketball team helped because the coach taught us a lot about hygiene.

Mother: Girls get pimples, too, but not usually as bad as some of the boys.

Jason: Did Julie get them?

Mother: Only a few. You see, we had a lot of talks like this while she was growing up, and she knew what to expect and what to do. We hope this works out well for you, too—the same way.

Dad: You are going to have some other things happen, too, like growing hair around your penis and testicles.

Jason: Well, I knew that—some of the older kids have hair down there and . . .

Mother: "Down there" is what we mean when we say "pubic hair."

Jason: Yes, I know that, we had pubic hair in hygiene and when you used to let Julie and me take showers together, she was getting some, too. That was quite a while ago, though . . .

Dad: And another thing—you've noticed that my penis and scrotum are bigger than yours?

Jason: Well, you're bigger all over, Dad.

Dad: I know, but different parts of your body grow at different speeds and times. What Mother and I want you to know is that you are going to get a spurt of growth and will change in your genital area.

Jason: I am? Gee, will it feel funny? When we use the locker room at school I notice some of the older kids have real big ones—but I thought they just grew bigger all over.

Dad: No, Jason, that all probably happened in the last year or two and within a year or less it will happen to you. And it won't feel funny—it happens so gradually that it's sort of fun. I can remember that I felt very grown up and used to show it off to your Uncle Charlie. He was two years older than I, and I was trying to catch up.

Mother: You *look* older than Charlie, dear.

Dad: Pay no attention to *that*, Jason! But there is something Mom told me that I think is important.

Jason: What's that?

Mother: Well, you noticed me washing out Julie's sheets last week and I explained to you about women's menstruating. Remember that—well—I want you to know about something that you might wake up and find in your sheets sometime.

Jason: Mom, I'm not a girl . . .

Mother: No, you are certainly not—but you soon will begin to have what we call nocturnal emissions, and they are perfectly normal and we don't want you frightened or worried or feeling that you have to keep it a secret.

Jason: What's a nock—nock . . .

Mother: Nocturnal emission. It means night—nocturnal just means happening in the nighttime—and emission means something coming out. They are also called "wet dreams."

Jason: Oh, I heard some of the kids talking about wet dreams, but I thought maybe they were dreaming about swimming or something.

Dad: No, they are talking about the sort of dream that is very sexually exciting and as a result they have an erection, you know, get a hard-on, and, right in their sleep, they may ejaculate a fluid from their penis.

Mother: What we want you to know is that's natural, it happens to every normal, growing boy. We expect it will

	happen to you sometime soon, and we want you to know about it in advance. So, when it happens, just tell me and I'll wash and dry your sheets—and you just take clean ones from the linen closet and make your bed up nice and dry and fresh.
Jason:	This sounds sort of weird. What's this stuff that's going to come out of my penis? I thought only pee came out of it. Is it bad? Will it hurt?
Dad:	None of those—it isn't bad and it doesn't hurt. As a matter of fact, it is a sort of new sensation that might even feel quite good, especially if you know about it in advance and know that it is just your body telling you that you are growing up and getting ready to be interested in girls and even in sex.
Jason:	Dad—girls are all right—but really, Dad . . .
Mother:	I know, Jason, and maybe we have talked enough for this time. Tell you what, take that book to your room—it's a good book about what happens to boys' bodies—and if you want to go any further with it tell Dad or me and we'll talk some more. Is that okay?

How would you grade the parents in the above illustration? We will return to this family to see how they handled some of the issues that Jason might raise after reading his book. Let's talk about Dad's performance in the illustration above. Dad, gets about a B for his performance. Maybe we can give him a B+ because he did one thing really well: He invited Mother into the discussion and he handed her the ball, so to speak, when he invited her to fill some openings he left, and also gave her a chance to bring her own contribution to the discussion.

Nancy gets an A. She and Henry planned well for this event, and with a little luck, it came off as planned. One of the ways you as parents can enhance your chances of teaching love along with sex is to get to the issues before they explode and you have a Vesuvius on your hands. That's why Nancy and Henry planned to be ahead of the game. They could set the scene, choose their opportunity, and manage it with warmth, care, and love. They were not forced to deal with clean-up after a tragedy. If parents only deal with kids' sexuality *after* a sexual event has occurred, you may be seen by your kids as paying attention to sex only when required. They will see you as firefighters rather than as "helpers." Let's take that one step further. If you give your kids attention only after a sexual goof, they just might, unconsciously, of course, use sex as an *attention-getting device.*

Another thought concerning planning ahead for sexual education is illustrated in our example. You noticed that Jason gave evidence of a little research he had done on his own. He knew some boys had "big ones," and he had heard something about wet dreams. The point is that you cannot control what your children will hear, when they will hear it, or how they will construe the meaning of what they hear. By bringing up the subject in a controlled situation, however, you do get a chance to learn what your child has experienced and how he interprets it. *And* he gets the message that you, as a parent, are an accepting resource for sexual information. As a result, he may even reduce some of his experimentation outside the house, or at least conduct those experiments with more information and understanding. So there may be even more benefits to loving, parental sexual education than meets the eye.

Let's get back to Henry and why he got marked down. When Jason, near the end of the talk, asked his Dad what it was that would come out of his penis in these nocturnal emissions, Dad did not answer that. He should have told Jason about semen, but instead Dad focused on the "pleasant sensation" part of the question. Perhaps what we are trying to illustrate here is that parents have to listen carefully and try to cover all the bases, although at another time they may get a second try. Kids are pretty forgiving in an atmosphere like the one Jason enjoys with his family: They can feel the good intentions and overlook the goofs.

Further Along on the Chart: Toward Puberty

Let's say that about ten months have passed since Henry and Nancy talked with their son. Jason has learned a lot in that length of time. He has read his book, Julie has noticed him reading it and has been a good older sister, telling him things he has asked. She had giggled with Mother about her "little brother's progress" and has pretty much shared these events with her mother. You might say she is identifying with her mother and the family openness, practicing for the motherhood that is probably ahead of her.

Jason is over ten years old now, and he has been watching his own development and that of the boys he sees in the showers and the locker room. He is proudly sporting a few straight little hairs around his genitals and under his arms.

Observing his own development is not all that positive for Jason. However, he decides to consult with his parents. We find him saying:

Jason: Mom and Dad—can I ask you something about my body and stuff, like you said I could?

Dad: Sure. What's up?

Mother: Is something troubling you? I've noticed you have been sort of quiet lately.

Jason: Well, it isn't some*thing*, really.

Mother: You're worrying about something. And you haven't been out playing with your friends as much as you used to—right? Or am I prying?

Jason: It's okay, Mom . . .

Dad: [*To Nancy*] You don't miss much, do you?

Jason: Yeah, Mom's sharp, Dad. She knows.

Dad: Okay, you two. Jason, how about letting me in on it? Your grandmother told me I had moods like this, too.

Jason: So that's where I get it. Okay, all right, but it's kind of weird and I don't know, but—you know—you guys gave me that book to read and I sort of can't get it out of my head.

Dad:	You worried about what will happen to you?
Jason:	No, Dad, it's not that I worry exactly, it's just that I'm thinking all the time and I don't mind the thinking, sometimes it's sort of fun—but—
Mother:	I have an idea of what you're thinking about, but perhaps you would rather say it yourself?
Dad:	Is there *anything* you haven't figured out yet?
Jason:	No, Mom. You would never guess this stuff—maybe I'm crazy or something but—I just keep thinking about *sexy stuff*!
Dad:	Easy, Jason, easy—let me reassure you—you are *not* crazy.
Jason:	Dad, some of the things I can keep seeing are just awful. I imagine—geez—boys and girls doing sexy things together and I don't know—
Mother:	I think your father told me about some of the scenes he used to think about when he was your age. I did that, too . . .
Jason:	*You* did, Mom? I can believe it about Dad—but Mom, you—a girl!
Mother:	I guess it's pretty normal for everybody to have these thoughts. We call them sexual fantasies.
Jason:	But, Dad, *I'm* in some of these fantasies, you call them. And what I do in them isn't nice. It isn't nice at all!
Dad:	Do you think it would help if you talked about them?
Jason:	No way!
Mother:	You don't have to. Dad was just letting you know that it can't be so bad that you can't talk about it. You can decide—after all, you own your own thoughts.
Dad:	Maybe one of the most personal things about it, and I remember this was true for me, is that these fantasies are sometimes associated with when you come off— you know, ejaculate.
Jason:	Yeah—you knew, huh, Dad? You know, sometimes you're as sharp as Mom, right?
Dad:	I try, Jason, I try.

Jason: Well, Dad—you told me it was all right to ejaculate, you know, but it's been happening more often. More than the other kids. They tell me it can affect me in all kinds of ways—and I don't know. Is that true?

Mother: No, it's not true at all. You probably saw in that book that it isn't harmful at all—it's natural and part of growing up.

Dad: As a matter of fact, Jason, Mother and I have been meaning to talk to you about another part of that whole problem, and maybe it's good you brought it up.

Jason: What other part?

Dad: Well, it has a big name, called "masturbation."

Jason: I know what that means. All the kids talk about it, and it was explained in the book and Julie told me, too.

Dad: Jason, are you telling us you are worried about masturbation?

Jason: No, Dad, you don't understand. I'm only ten—well, almost eleven—you know. I'm worried about what I catch myself thinking about. I told you. You called it fantasies. Dad, I don't masturbate or jerk off or whatever you call it. I just *think*.

Mother: Would you like some help on how to stop those thoughts—or at least reduce or control them better?

Jason: You mean there is something I can do to stop what I think? Really? Is it hard?

Mother: Well, yes, there is—and it's related to what I said earlier—that you were quiet and not going out to play with your friends. It's not hard, in fact, it sounds so easy you may not think it will work. But I guarantee you that if you do it, it *will* work.

Jason: Okay, so what do I do?

Mother: Two things. The first one is called "thought stopping." Whenever you want to stop what you are thinking, just imagine you see a great big STOP sign—like the one at the end of our street—and yell "Stop!" Of course, you only yell out loud if you are alone. If people are around, just sort of yell it to yourself, see . . .

Jason: It's okay, Mom, I get it—but what's the second thing? You said there were two.

Mother: The other is easier, and harder. Just get out and do something, especially if you can find other kids or anybody to do it with. Even us.

Jason: But, that's just the point. I don't feel like it.

Dad: That *is* the point, son. Mother is suggesting that you are getting kind of moody and alone. I want to make it clear to you that we understand that, and we know it is part of the changes you are going through. Maybe something else is happening, too. Maybe you are enjoying being with your sister and her friends. I notice you sort of stay around when she has them over here.

Jason: Well, I don't know, Dad—it's not exactly that. Some of them are real nice, but I sure don't like Alice!

Mother: But, Jason, how about my two suggestions? Maybe they would fit right in with what Dad is saying?

Jason: Well, okay, Mom. I'll try the thought stopping, but I don't know about getting out more. The kids don't seem to want me around.

Mother: You know, Jason, sometimes when we feel that others are rejecting us, we are really distancing *ourselves* from *them*.

Jason: You're always blaming me.

Dad: I don't think Mother is blaming you, Jason. I think she is just trying to help you understand some of the funny things that happen in our heads—especially when we feel that we are behaving strangely. So maybe the best way to help you out of this funk is to assure you that you really are okay, you are *not* weird, but going through something that happens to all children as they grow up.

Jason: Well, you make it all sound so okay. I can't quite believe all that quite yet, though.

Mother: Jason, I have a good idea. Let me drive you down to the playground. Just try it out.

There is a time to end conversations, and obviously Nancy felt that the time had come. There is also a time to switch from words to action, and Nancy made that switch. She felt Jason was talked out and that handling two adults was a bit much for him. So, with a wink at Henry, she made her move and it worked. Jason needed out!

Let's look further into this parenting scene and see what we can extract from it.

Mother noticed Jason had been "sort of quiet lately." She knew that a child's moods are important messages transmitted in an indirect way. This is especially true *before* the age of twelve. Children under twelve usually have a hard time dealing with anything abstract—like sadness, optimism, or profit. They have not yet adequately developed the ability to handle concepts, and they often lack the vocabulary to do so. Also, they have not developed insight skills to see themselves in a situation. They just react.

Jason is a good example. Since he could not verbally handle his troubles, he unconsciously used his mood to telegraph a message that something was wrong. Nancy picked up the message and moved in when he gave her an opening. If she had asked him earlier, "Why are you sulking—why don't you go out and play?" our guess is that Jason would not have been able to answer. He has enough trouble identifying and labeling his symptoms; he certainly cannot yet explain them. He lacks the capacity to abstract, and he lacks the insight and the vocabulary.

Therefore, one of the benefits of talking openly and warmly with your children about sex and love is that parents get an idea of where their children are in the process of identifying and handling concepts and feelings. In addition, the kids get an opportunity to learn how to do that in a safe, secure atmosphere.

A little further on, Nancy employs deliberate self-revelation when she says, "Your father told me about some of the scenes he used to think about when he was your age. I did that, too." Note how she does it: She cites what Father said because she thinks Jason can identify better with a man who has gone through what Jason is experiencing. She also models sharing for Jason by showing that Dad told *her*. Then she shows her willingness for self-revelation with the simple statement that she did that, too. Nancy is modeling her belief that these subjects are best dealt with out in the open.

One of the best ways to build trust is with self-revelation. Why? Because if I volunteer my secrets to you, I am showing that I trust you. If you feel trusted by me, you can more easily return that trust. It's a question of who dares to go first. Nancy shows Jason that both she and Dad are willing to go first. That made it easier for Jason to share that what he did in his fantasies wasn't "nice at all."

Please also notice that Nancy does not *push* for revelation but builds Jason's autonomy by telling him that she respects his decision. Her words "you own your own thoughts" project that respect and recognize a powerful reality: We are not able to get into our kids' heads. Nancy avoids being a parental "detective." She avoids identity-smashing remarks like "Mother always knows what you are thinking."

Henry knows that as well—and he just stays easily with it and, continuing to use self-revelation, brings up the very delicate subject of masturbation.

Nice teamwork by two caring parents!

Dad makes one more deep exploration: "Maybe you are enjoying being with your sister and her friends?" Dad is testing the possibility that Jason just might be getting interested in girls. Maybe Jason is learning about more mature girls from his older sister. When Jason fails to bite, Dad drops it, and Mother moves in with her offer of action and an opportunity to end the conversation.

Check the Chart: Where We Have Been and Where We're Going

We can easily see that the preteen age covers a great deal of what is on the chart. We feel this period is important because it gives parents the opportunity to anticipate their children's need for sexual information and guidance. If you can get in there ahead of the crisis, you have the problem at least half licked.

In the preceding dialogues and discussions, we have talked about most of the material on the chart: general physical development, sexual physical development, and some of the emotional development. We will want to talk more about that, and to go on with some discussion about menstruation, lovemaking, and how you make your values clear to your child. We will also deal with friendship and peer pressure.

Talking About Menstruation

Menstruation is a miraculous event. If we think about how complex and beautifully constructed our bodies are, and how efficiently they work, we can see that it's marvelous. And if we can convey that kind of celebration to our girls and boys, it would be wonderful. It might encourage them to take good care of themselves. The inner timetable that we all contain is nothing short of dazzling. Think of the number of women in this world, past and present, who have on some hidden signal begun to grow pubic hair, experience growing breasts, and then have a menstrual cycle. Each has had her own timetable. Some begin as young as eight years old, some don't begin until sixteen. But the miracle is that within those eight years, just about every healthy female has experienced this change of maturity.

Since some girls do begin to menstruate at the age of

eight, that seems like a good time to prepare them. There are usually signs that their bodies are getting ready to develop. Some straggly pubic hair appears. Some hair begins to show under the arms. Breasts begin to enlarge. These are all visible signs of growing maturity. Ovulation only makes its presence known with the menses, which means that our daughters are biological women and able to bear children.

At the age of eight, how much do our daughters need to know? Fifty years ago they would have been told that once a month they were going to bleed and to wear a napkin when that happens. They might have been told to avoid sports and bathing during this time. They might have been told, "You are now a woman"—and not to talk about it.

Thirty years ago they were told about their internal organs and how they all played a part in producing menstruation. They might have been congratulated on achieving a significant time of life. They were certainly encouraged to take sports and baths, but every girl knew that if she went to the gym teacher and complained, she could get out of taking gym. But with the growing popularity of female sports stars, who continue to perform and compete regardless of what their bodies are doing, there is a new model available to our daughters and their gym teachers. Our teaching is now that menstruation is a normal part of life, and life goes on accordingly. In addition to a changed attitude, we also supply more information about the way bodies operate and we include a brief explanation of how babies are conceived. Considering the number of teenage pregnancies, it seems wise to provide our young ones with total information.

Another significant change is that we now tell boys about what puberty means to girls, just as we tell girls how boys experience puberty. Menstruation and erections are no longer secrets. Our new attitude is that every part of the body is wholesome and respectable. There is nothing secret or dirty about any of it. What our children must learn to do is to use their bodies wisely and well.

Fifty years ago, the menstrual period was treated like a secret event. Fathers pretended they never knew what was going on. Certainly brothers didn't. It was something between mothers and daughters, and even then it was barely referred to. It always amazed us that sisters who shared bedrooms seldom shared information about their periods. It was a time of pretending it just wasn't happening. Now we suggest that fathers and mothers talk to their daughters and sons about sexual maturation, thus returning the whole subject to normalcy. Perhaps just as they learned to ride a bicycle, so your children will learn about puberty. In other words, we want our children to know that puberty is normal. Everyone goes through it. There's nothing shameful or secretive about it. It's really a wonderful demonstration that our bodies are normal and doing what they're supposed to be doing.

We're going to envision a mother and daughter talking. Perhaps they're doing a task together, such as washing the dishes. Perhaps they're driving somewhere. Maybe they're just eating together. At any rate, Mom has left plenty of time for this discussion because she wants to cover a lot of information and have plenty of time for questions. So it might go like this.

Mom:	My goodness, Samantha, you're growing so fast. Didn't I just buy you those new slacks? You're almost out of them.
Samantha:	I know it, and next time I want some red ones like Janie's.
Mom:	Not only are you going to need some new slacks, but I want you to know what else is going to happen to you as you get older and bigger.
Samantha:	You mean like more allowance? Janie gets more allowance now.
Mom:	Well, I didn't have allowances in mind just now. What I was thinking about was your body.
Samantha:	What's wrong with it?

Mom:	Not a thing. It's doing beautifully and I'm delighted to see that. It's doing just what it's supposed to, and I want to tell you what it's going to be doing next.
Samantha:	What do you mean?
Mom:	Well, pretty soon you're going to find more hair growing on your body—under your arms and between your legs. It will start out with just a few hairs, but as you get older, your hair will get darker and bushier and kinkier.
Samantha:	Why?
Mom:	That's a good question. Everyone—Mom, Dad, your teachers, Grandpa, and Nana—everyone has a kind of timetable in her or his body which starts the kind of development that I'm going to tell you about. When the time comes, hormones begin to pour into your body from your pituitary gland, which is in your brain. Those hormones tell your hair on your body to start growing. They also tell your breasts to start growing.
Samantha:	You mean I'd wear bras like yours?
Mom:	Well, that won't happen for a while yet so let's not worry about it. Let's concentrate on the miracle of your growing.
Samantha:	Isn't that enough?
Mom:	Nope. A lot more is going to happen, if you're going to be like other girls. It's really miraculous.
Samantha:	What?
Mom:	Remember when you wanted to know how babies came, and we told you that lovingly men insert their penises into women's vaginas? And then men ejaculate sperm into the vagina which then travel up to the uterus. If the woman has an egg in her uterus that meets with the sperm, then a baby can get started. Remember my telling you that? And you wanted to know if it hurt and I said no, it was a warm and loving thing to do with someone you loved. Remember all that?
Samantha:	Sort of. I guess I remember now.

Mom: Good. Because now I want to tell you the rest of the story. Let's say the egg and the sperm meet and the egg is fertilized. Your body then prepares to take care of this fertilized egg and builds a kind of nest for it in the uterus so that the baby will grow. You know it takes nine months for the baby to grow. That's why you see some women with very big tummies. Their babies are getting bigger and bigger until they are ready to be born.

Samantha: Well, Mom, what happens if the egg is not fertilized?

Mom: Oh, honey, you do ask the best questions. If the egg is not fertilized, then the thick lining of the uterus, which grew in order to protect the egg, flows out of the woman's body, sort of like urine, only it comes in the form of blood. It takes anywhere from five to seven days to stop, and it happens about once a month."

Samantha: Well, how do you keep your pants clean?

Mom: We have pads or tampons that we can wear to protect ourselves. Later I will take you upstairs and show them to you. Tomorrow we'll go down to the drugstore and buy a supply for you, since we want you to be ready.

Samantha: Mom, does that mean you do that?

Mom: If by 'that' you mean do I still menstruate, the answer is yes. Many women continue to have periods of menstruation until they are in their fifties.

Samantha: I didn't know you did that.

Mom: Well, honey, I'm only in my forties."

Samantha: What happens if you don't have periods?

Mom: That's one way of knowing whether or not you're pregnant. That means that the egg could have been fertilized. Or it could mean that I'm getting to the time when I will no longer have periods. That's called menopause.

Samantha: Can people tell when you're having a period?

Mom: No. I'm having one right now. Could you tell?

Samantha: No. Does Aunt Alice have periods?

Mom: Yes.

Samantha:	How about Grandma?
Mom:	No. I think she wouldn't. I think she would be in menopause now. That means no periods and no more babies.
Samantha:	Do boys have periods?
Mom:	No. Only girls, because only girls can have babies. Once a girl starts having periods, she could even start a baby.
Samantha:	Mom, do you mean if I had a period, I could have a baby?
Mom:	Not unless the egg were fertilized by a boy, and you're in charge of letting a boy put his penis in your vagina. So I think you won't be having babies in a hurry. But that's a very good question.
Samantha:	Well, shouldn't boys have to do something?
Mom:	You mean, how do boys grow up?
Samantha?	Yeah.
Mom:	Their voices change. They get more hair on their faces, too. You've seen Daddy shaving. And their penis and testicles grow bigger. As a matter of fact, sometimes their penis gets big when they don't even want it to, and they say that it is very embarrassing. Dad could tell you more about that. We'll ask him after dinner.
Samantha:	Does anything else happen to boys?
Mom:	Yes, their breasts get bigger, but girls' breasts are always bigger than men's. When they get old enough, girls usually wear bras because it is more comfortable. You've seen mine. Someday you will wear something like that."
Samantha:	What else?
Mom:	Really, that's about it. When your period starts, the only difference it will make is that you will have to wear something to protect yourself from the flow of blood. Otherwise, you'll never know anything has happened. It's really an exciting time because you will know that your body is doing everything it is supposed to be doing. Nature is really remarkable. You know, Daddy is an engineer and knows

how to make things work. But he couldn't have done a better job at constructing our bodies if he'd tried. Do you have any more questions?

Samantha: No, I don't think so.

Mom: Okay. But whenever you do, come and talk to me about them. I love talking with you.

This is an example of a wonderful mother and daughter, very communcative and sharing. But suppose you clear the decks to talk to your daughter and she just isn't in the mood? You can see that she isn't taking in a word you're saying. That happens. Don't get discouraged. Just try again when the stars and the moon are in a different configuration, or whatever it takes to get your child's attention. You might try another tack by showing her a napkin and a tampon and asking her if she knows what they are and what they are for.

That seems like a lot of information to relay for the first time. On another occasion, particularly if you have a friend who is nursing a baby, or a pet that is nursing, you might explain the function of breasts. For example, you might say, "After the baby is born, the breasts fill with milk, so the babies can 'nurse' or drink. Babies are born without teeth and so the only way they can get food is to suck either a breast or a nipple on a bottle filled with special milk."

Many girls wonder if they have to have big breasts in order to make milk. The answer, of course, is no. Women with all sizes of breasts can nurse their babies.

One way of repeating this information is to explain it again when a girl your daughter knows gets her period. It gives you a rather natural way to keep reintroducing the information so that when your daughter's time comes, she is fully prepared and not embarrassed.

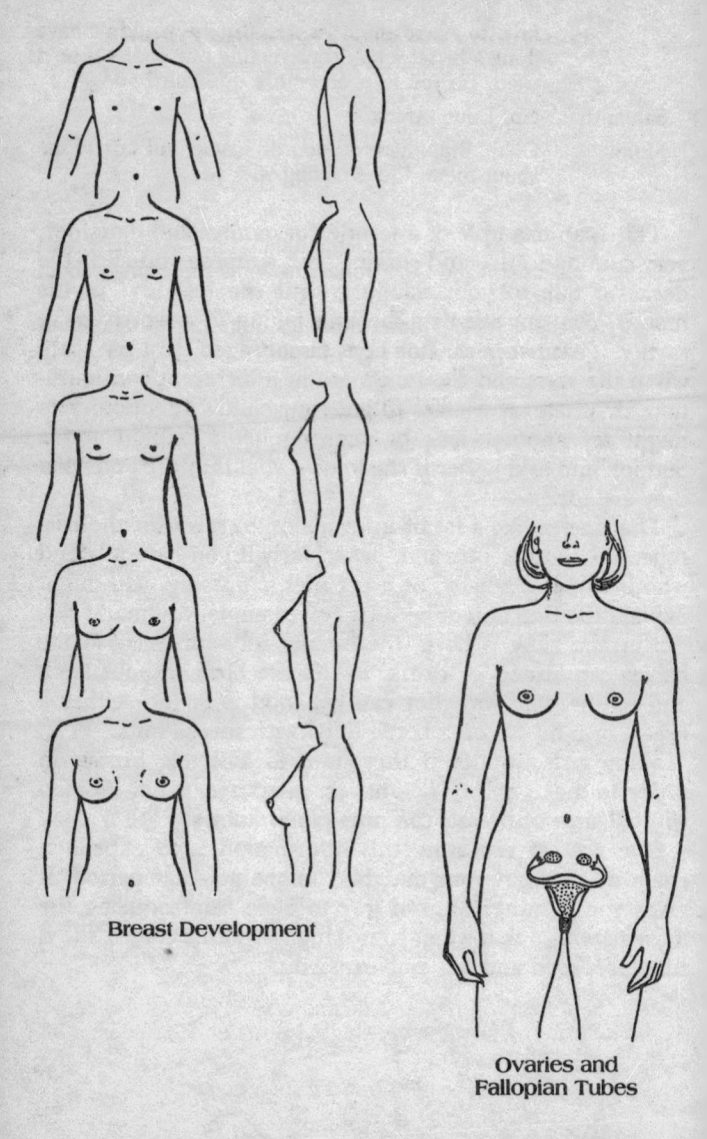

Breast Development

Ovaries and
Fallopian Tubes

Teaching One Sex About the Other: Nancy Tells Jason About Menstruation

Remember our friend Jason and his mother, Nancy, sister, Julie, and father, Henry? Nancy told us about a talk she had with Jason when they were alone one day. It went like this:

Jason: Ma, can I ask you something? Julie isn't here this afternoon and I was wondering about something—about Julie.

Nancy: About Julie? I don't think it's quite fair to talk about her when she isn't here, Jason.

Jason: No, Mother, it's not something like that. I just wanted to know something and you said I could ask anytime. It's not a secret or squealing or anything like that.

Nancy: Well, try me—but if it isn't fair, we'll have to talk with Julie.

Jason: Well, she keeps those white tubes or something in the medicine cabinet in our bathroom, and there isn't much room in there. I asked her to keep them somewhere else and she said she had to have them in the bathroom.

Nancy: Did you ask her why she needs them in there?

Jason: No, she said she was in a hurry and would explain it to me some other time.

Nancy: Some other time . . .

Jason: Well, that's what's so funny, Mom—she said if I couldn't wait, I could ask you and it would be all right if you told me. Told me what, Mom? You tell me to ask anything, and she tells me to ask you, and I don't know what's going on around here.

Nancy: I'm sorry, dear. I'll tell you right now. It goes like this: Those "tubes" in the medicine cabinet are called tampons. Girls, when they reach puberty, manufacture a tiny egg with the ovary we showed you in that illustration some time ago. Do you remember it?

Jason: Well, vaguely. Can I go and get the book and then we can follow those drawings? I don't quite remember all this stuff, you know.

Nancy: Sure—get the book and I'll show you . . .

Nancy guided Jason through the pages on menstruation. She did so, knowing that Jason was now ready to absorb and hold this information. They had skimmed it before, and both Nancy and Henry did not emphasize it too much then because Jason's attention span was waning at the time. They knew that he was either tired or overloaded with starting new information and that another time would come. This was the time, and Nancy decided that she would try to take advantage of this "readiness" to teach Jason about pregnancy and sexual intercourse. Also, the subjects followed each other nicely: Discussion about ovulation could precede learning about fertilization. The "big moment" was at hand.

Nancy: Jason, I've shown you how a woman makes an egg and how that *unfertilized* egg plays a part in menstruation, right?

Jason: So what happens if it's fertilized? And what do you mean by fertilized, anyway? I know you put fertilizer in your plants—but what is this?

Nancy: This kind of fertilization is a real miracle; it is how life starts.

Jason: You mean, this is how babies are started? You know, I have been wondering about that and so have some of the other kids.

Nancy: Well, here goes. A woman's egg is fertilized by a sperm from a man. You remember how we told you that the discharge from a boy's penis contains sperm?

Jason: You mean in those wet dreams we talked about?

Nancy: Right. And you remember we talked about erections, when your penis gets hard?

Jason: I don't have to remember—it happens a lot now.

Nancy: Well, there is a purpose for that hardness. That makes it possible to insert the penis into the vagina.

Jason: But why would anyone want to do that? Why would a girl let a boy do it?

Nancy: That's a good question. It might be hard for you to understand it now, but when people are feeling warm and loving, and when the penis and the area around the vagina are fondled— you know, stroked and touched—there are nerves that send a message telling the brain that it feels good. In fact, when a woman feels this pleasure, she has the female equivalent of an erection. Her vagina opens and produces a fine, slippery fluid and that makes it possible for the penis to slip right in.

Jason: What happens then—how does the egg get fertilized?

Nancy: Well, the man ejaculates and sometimes one of the sperm from the man contacts the egg produced by the woman's ovary, and the two get together and start, would you believe, a baby!

Jason: So that's where the stuff—semen—that my testicles make, and comes out of my penis—that's where it's *supposed* to go? And you told me that the semen contains sperm?

Nancy: That's right. That's what fertilizes the egg—if it meets up with an egg that's ready. That's how babies are started.

Jason: But how does the boy know he is supposed to come—uh—to ejaculate?

Nancy: Good—you got the right word. You remember I just mentioned how pleasant a sensation it is? Well, when men are pleasured that way, they reach ejaculation naturally.

Jason: Sounds like everything was sort of—planned . . .

Nancy: It is wonderful, isn't it? Wonderful planning—the way our bodies work. But making babies is a big responsibility, and Dad and I will need to talk to you about that someday. It's a big subject for you to understand when you get a little older. I've only told you enough for a beginning, really. There is lots more to learn.

Explaining Erection and Its Function in Intercourse

Let's get acquainted with Walter, his son, Peter, and his daughter, Paula. Walter works outdoors most of the time and enjoys using his body. He is good at sports and likes baseball in the summer and indoor tennis in the winter. Peter is thirteen years old and admires his father. He loves to go with Dad on Saturday morning in the new pickup truck that Dad prefers to the family car. Paula, eleven, also enjoys these Saturday mornings. She looks forward to Saturdays as her chance to be out with the men doing big, adult things.

Walter is in charge of the family on Saturday and he enjoys both giving his wife a chance to sleep in and having the kids to himself. It's eight o'clock and they will all have breakfast at Joe's Diner, the last truck stop left outside of town.

The truck rides hard as they bump along on the old back road. Walter takes short cuts, and the rougher the terrain the better chance to put the new vehicle to the test. After about five minutes of this, he notices that Peter is squirming uncomfortably.

Walter:	What's the matter, Pete? Does this new truck ride a little too hard for you?
Peter:	No—uh—it's not the new truck, Dad. It's just that I got these new jeans on and with the bumps and things I—ah— well, you know, Dad!
Walter:	Well, I really don't know, son, but I'll slow down and maybe it will be easier on you.
Peter:	That won't do it, but thanks anyway. It will go away after we get out—it always does.
Paula:	What will go away? What always does, Peter?
Peter:	Paula, it doesn't go away, really. This is sort of different and Dad will understand, but I don't know about you—you're a girl.

Walter: I get it now, Peter. You remember what we all agreed to at that family meeting we had? Mom and I told you both that boys get to know about girls' bodies and girls get to learn about boys just as well.

Peter: I know, Dad, but it's kind of embarrassing.

Walter: Sure it is—but it's also natural. So let me help you out with this, okay?

Peter: Well, you can tell her—but I don't know . . .

Paula: Tell me what, Dad?

Walter: Tell you that your brother is uncomfortable because his penis has got all hard like Mom and I showed you in that book about sex. That's right, Peter, isn't it?

Peter: You got it, Dad. Now that you remind me about that time we all talked together, I guess it isn't so bad if Paula knows.

Paula: Really, Peter, it isn't much different than you knowing that some day I'm going to—uh—mensrate?

Walter: Pretty close, honey—the word is "menstruate." And the word for hard penis is "erection."

Paula: Okay. But does it hurt, Peter? You seem very uncomfortable.

Peter: Sure it hurts! But not really—sort of. It's just that I can't seem to control it and whenever it gets cramped or rubbed, like the car seat is doing now, I get a hard-on and it needs room to stretch out, and sometimes my pants won't let it and I'm sure everybody is going to see the bump in my pants, and it's awful!

Walter: That's right, I can remember, Peter, that I used to sneak my hand in my pocket and hold it down so I could stand up and run around until it went down. But I got so red in the face, I guess I didn't hide too much one way or another.

Paula: I think it's worse for girls when they mens-tru-ate because we have to wear pads and everything.

Walter: Kind of tough on you both, huh?

Peter: I sort of scrunched up my pants when I jumped in here. Maybe if I could just pull them down, like this— there, that helps.

Paula: I don't know why you're embarrassed. All I can see is a few wrinkles.

Walter: See that—an unbiased witness. I'll bet you're feeling better already, Peter.

Peter: Yup. And you know, Dad, as we talk I get relaxed and it always goes down then.

Walter: Sure, that's half the battle, son. Try your best to think of something else—something funny if you can—and you'll soften right up.

Paula: I've heard the boys at school call it a "boner". Does your penis have a bone in it? How could it get soft if it did?

Peter: No, that's not what we learned in hygiene class. It's different. Sort of like a sponge made up of lots of tiny spaces where the blood can fill up the spaces and make it seem hard as a bone.

Walter: You know, Paula, you asked a good question. I didn't really understand what caused an erection until I was about twenty. The kids had all kinds of crazy explanations. And all that mystery about girls menstruating! It was your mother who really gave me the word on that one. When she got pregnant with you, Peter, we went to classes together and that is where I resolved that *my* kids were not going to grow up uninformed like me.

Paula: Well, okay—if you were going to "inform" us, maybe you can explain something I still don't understand. You told us that sex was a boy putting his penis into a girl's vagina, right?

Walter: That's about as simple as you can describe it. Yup, that's right. Now what's your question?

Paula: How does a boy get something that big into that little space? It doesn't make sense, Dad.

Walter: Well, it does seem impossible, but two things have to happen—no, three. The first is that erection we are talking about. That has to happen and it does because sexual excitement, loving, warmth, and all those nice things cause erections. The next two things have to happen to the girl and they do happen if she also feels warm and loving.

Paula: What are those two things?

Peter: Yeah, I've wondered about this, too. What are they, Dad?

Walter: Well, bodies *are* wonderful things, you know. The woman's body actually makes a fluid that is like a fine oil, which lubricates her vagina. The second thing is that the vagina actually opens wider, wide enough so that the penis fits just right and slides in on that nice, fine oil. And it feels good for both of them—fine and loving and special. Guess I'm getting carried away a bit here.

Peter: So maybe getting a hard-on is a good thing some day, huh, Dad?

Walter: Yes, kids, when you combine all that with loving that one special person you want to spend all your life with, you bet it's special! Now, who's for a real big breakfast?

Did you approve of how Walter handled that talk with his children? Perhaps you felt he was too open, and that in real life such a scene could never take place? Or perhaps you felt that he went too far with the children and that he lacks sensitivity?

Your concerns would be justified if Walter did this out of nowhere without the background of earlier talks that he indicates did take place. Sex education, especially education about loving sex, cannot take place successfully in a vacuum. It cannot be done as a single event, or a string of isolated, unrelated events. And it cannot be effective in an emotional refrigerator. There has to be sexual history, and Walter certainly has clear, ringing values. He did not take the kids out for a ride in order to deliver a lecture on sex. He takes them every Saturday because he loves them. They go because they love him. There is a continuity of warmth and trust, including sexual education, which has been going on since the kids were three and learned about good touching versus bad touching. With trust and warmth, parents who know their own history and values can successfully teach loving sex to sons and daughters at the same time. And they can teach their sons about girls and their daughters about boys.

Explaining and Dealing With Emotions

We have discussed general physical development and sexual physical development. Next we come to emotional development. We have talked about our children's bodies and how they function and develop sexually. Now we are going to focus more on emotions, which may be a little more difficult for parents to understand and to manage. Body changes affect the children more directly because they see and experience them consciously. They are acutely aware of what is happening to them. But children lack insight and don't monitor their feelings that way.

Also, children usually don't understand how difficult it is for parents to see them suffer emotional pain. It's hard to watch a daughter cry over being rejected by the boy on whom she has a crush. And, as all parents know, children frequently direct their emotions directly at their parents. That's a lot harder to take from your preteen than it was from your five-year-old.

So, to be most helpful, we are going to focus first on helping parents *expect* and *understand* preteen emotional development. Second, we are going to suggest some ways of handling these emotional outbursts so that they become both a productive learning experience and an opportunity for teaching safer, loving sexuality. That might turn out to be a bit ambitious, but let's try it.

We will be using the words "feelings" and "emotions" a great deal in this section, and we would like to ask you to accept our meaning for them here. "Feelings" and "emotions" will refer to sensations like sadness, joy, anger, compassion, fury, despair, or disappointment. Feelings are not, in this context, opinions. for example, the statement "I feel that the Democrats will win" is an expression of opinion. We will use the word neither to indicate touch, as in "feel how soft it is," nor to indicate physical state, as in "I feel faint."

It is really helpful to expect and understand emotional

changes. We recall reading Dr. Benjamin Spock some decades ago, and what a relief it was to know that we could expect our baby to seem friendly to strangers until she could distinguish them from familiar figures. It kept us from worrying about her "emotional development" at three months of age! Even more reassuring was understanding the discussion of the "terrible twos," when our sweet child became a temporary tyrant.

So, take heart. The preteen emotional roller coaster is a normal developmental process. It is not a unique, aberrant pattern of behavior that your child has contrived for your exquisite torture. And, even though she may aim those feelings straight at you, try to hang on and understand that you are not the real target. You are a "safe" target," the person at whom she can try out—dump out—those overwhelming, strange new feelings welling up inside. She has to get them out first. Then, after they are vented, you and she can deal with them.

Girls

Let's start with the girls. The chart indicates that preteen girls have strong sexual feelings, and if you have a daughter this age, we are sure this is no news to you. Those feelings probably start as undefined stirrings, which gradually define themselves as peers talk together, as the media provide erotic examples, and as other stimuli enter into her life. She begins to fantasize about sex and love, and then talk about it with trusted friends. You've already overheard those long telephone conversations about how Jimmy has a crush on Susie and Johnny caught them kissing! The fantasies get a little nearer to reality as daughter selects some boy she "loves" and tells all her girlfriends. However, she has never spoken to him except once in the lunch line! Elaborate plots are devised, telling Jane that Billy has a crush on her to see if Jane will talk to Billy who has admitted to being smitten—from what he thought was a safe distance. These are hard times, especially in social situations where girls are not supposed to initiate relations with boys.

The next step might be some action—"acting out," as it's called in the professional jargon. There might be some flirting, some hand-holding, spending time together, horse-play (especially on the beach), and even some kissing and safe physical contact—like hugging. Thus it goes from vague stirrings, to fantasy, to talk, and finally, to action. Many forms of human behavior travel the same route.

How might parents productively respond to these developments? We suggest that you take a loving, understanding stance. Please don't think we confuse love and understanding with passive condoning of behavior that is unacceptable to you. Not at all, not anywhere in this book. Hold your values and limits steady. If you don't want kids petting on your couch, don't permit it. If you want your daughter in at ten, demand it. Kids need structure, rules, and limits, but they do better if understanding and love show right through the firmness. All we are recommending is that you try to make your position clear. Take your daughter aside and try something like this:

> "Janie, I want you to know something. I think your strong feelings for Jimmy are natural and wonderful. I can imagine the excitement you feel when you are with him. And I know you want to hold and cherish him. Dad also understands, and we both are proud to see you developing into a loving young woman. We love you for being able to love, and we don't mean to keep you for ourselves, or hold you back, or any of those things. It's just that Dad and I have our own values and feel that those are best for you to follow while you are at this age. We want you to learn to love safely, with dignity, and with pride in your own body and standards. We want you to be able to look back at these years without regret. So we will insist that you follow our rules. That's our way of being helpful."

Although we urge parents to take a firm stance, we also recognize reality and understand that parents *cannot* always control their children's behavior. Please be gentle with yourselves if your son or daughter does not follow your firm, loving counsel. It is not necessarily your fault; if you feel you have done all you can in a reasonable way and your child still does her own thing, have some compassion for yourself and hold the child, not yourself, responsible for the consequences of her actions. Perhaps a simple axiom, a simple reality would help: You cannot control another person's actions unless you physically overpower them. Think about it a bit. And even if you do overpower them, there is a limit to what you can *make* them do. Some days, you can't even make them take out the garbage.

We also recommend that you don't get uptight and that you avoid hysteria or overreaction. Your outbursts will show your child that she controls the magic button that turns on your emotions. Then you become a nifty toy for your child to play with. She can turn Mom or Dad on or off at will!

So defuse situations by refusing to get sucked into a contest of emotions. Instead, be open to talk about what is going on. Use self-revelation—especially about your own goofs, rather than your success at being a "good girl" when you were young. Tell about the pain and consequences of those goofs. Ask your daughter to name the feelings she experiences, and show your empathy for her feelings.

We would like to suggest a hint about communications technique. After you show your understanding, don't ever use a phrase beginning with "*but* _____." Just substitute "*and* _____." Example:

"I understand *but* I still want you to come right home." The message is: My understanding is canceled by my demand that you come right home. Whereas:
"I understand *and* I still want you to come right home." The message is: My understanding is sincere and still I demand that you come right home.

Another way of dealing with stronger sexual feelings is to encourage your daughter's association with healthy friends and activities. Healthy friends and healthy activities go together. You can probably get more control by focusing on the activities instead of abstract issues. If you say, "Why don't you play with Janie—she is such a nice girl?" you may get a flip response. If, however, you say, "Janie's mother and I have tickets for you two for the figure skating next week," you may have more luck.

Mood Shifts

You have undoubtedly seen your preteen daughter go from being warm and playful to acting downright witchy— and all in a matter of minutes. You have probably seen desperate sadness replaced by instant joy. You may have witnessed her rapid transition from passive to aggressive, from dominant to submissive, from cold distancing to inappropriate overrelating, from disdainful to fawning. She can be agreeable at lunch and hostile at dinner. She can be excited when it is time for bed, and listless in the morning. She can be benevolent with her friend and selfish to her little brother. She is dejected at a football game and laughs at the death scene in the movie. She trusts the biggest cheat on the street and is paranoid about generous Aunt Mary.

If an adult showed such shifts in feelings, we would properly wonder about her mental health. But not with our preteen daughter; she is just learning, testing, experimenting—in other words, growing. All the body changes related to her sexuality that we reviewed above are showing in her emotional responses. If we can accept that, we can get a clue about managing to live with her. The method is easy to state, harder to do: Give her your *permission* to have her feelings.

If you try to calm her when she is excited, or enliven her when she is depressed, she may not see that as helpful. We know you mean it to be—who likes to see an unhappy or out-of-control child? But she may see it as interference with her rights to her own feelings. That happens on Tuesdays. On Friday your solace may be welcomed with gushing tears of appreciation. So if you give her the right to have her feelings, letting her know that you are there to help, or stay away as she may desire, you avoid getting your own feelings tossed about like a cork on a wave. Sexual development is literally a body in motion; don't try to stop it, just try to influence its direction.

Another step in dealing with preteen moods is to refuse to take responsibility for them. Suppose your daughter (or anybody) says something like: "Leave me alone—whenever you tell me it's better, you *make* me feel worse." Your response could be something like: "No, I don't make you feel anything. You choose to respond to my efforts by feeling worse. You are in charge of your feelings and they are not automatic. You are the owner of your moods." That's pretty strong stuff, but it is real. Because it is strong, you might want to apply it gently, much more gently than the example above. But, firmly or gently, don't get blackmailed into feeling guilty and responsible. Feeling inadequate to change our child's developing world is hard enough. Just hang on to your good intentions; normal children eventually come around to perceiving that.

Preteen Tension and Anxiety

Tension and anxiety are like extra emotional weights added to a task. We like the word "valence" as a description of that weight. Preteens add valence to situations and tasks that don't seem to have any. "I can't wash my hair, it makes me furious!" Everything is hard, or slow, or fast. They find more stimuli for tension than we could possibly imagine. Choices make them tense, decisions are hard, appetite varies, sleep is evasive, and when it comes, waking is horrendous. Your preteen will hang on to problems and accept no solution. It is almost as if she wants the problem to remain unsolved. This is especially true when the problems are related to her body. Nothing feels good: The new bra feels funny, the deodorant irritates her skin, tampons are unnatural, and pads are worse; boys are just awful!

What to do about it? First, accept the behavior and don't escalate the tension by adding your own. Kids perceive your need to get them to relax as something you have to endure with at least as much pain as they are feeling. If you accept their behavior, with compassion and kindness, of course, then you don't get caught in the loop. She will probably reject or refuse your offer to help. If you suggest she stop seeing Johnny since she complains that he always tries to kiss her, she accuses you of inhibiting her normal development. Withdraw your offer graciously and, as we suggest above, give your permission to your daughter to have and to hold her own tension. Then make yourself invisible—a very handy gimmick for all parents.

Concentration

Girls generally learn to concentrate earlier and probably better than most boys. As we have suggested above, at about the age of twelve children develop the capacity to think in abstractions. As thought processes improve, concentration becomes more productive and rewarding. Reading and even studying (required reading with learning and memorization) get more pleasurable. In school, the rewards are strong and the reinforcement flows out of teachers, friends, and parents. The girls see themselves outperforming the boys scholastically. They love having an area of superiority after years of knuckling under to boys' bigger bodies and superior physical strength. They know, too, that their body development and their sexuality are ahead of the boys, and they start looking for older boys who can match their intellectuality and warm, exciting feelings.

Perceptual Distortion and Defensiveness

When your daughter was five years old, she might have said something like, "My teddy bear just hit my dolly, Elizabeth. You better scold him." That was not perceptual distortion, that was fantasy. Fantasy is a deliberate, conscious separation from reality in which we allow our imagination free reign to create something different from reality. We know we are doing it.

When your daughter was seven, she might have secretly eaten the last three cookies in the jar and, when asked, denied doing so. Of course, you might have seen the overwhelming evidence all over her face. Her lie was not perceptual distortion; she knew what she had done. She lied to change reality in her favor. Children are pretty powerless, and when things are bad, they naively attempt to change reality by reporting it to be different from what it is.

However, when your preteen daughter says that her older sister only goes out with Peter to make her jealous, that is probably a distortion of reality, perceiving it as it is not. She wants to be grown up, and it pains her to see her sister going out with this man who is ten years older than she is.

Let's go one step further to get to defensiveness. If that same preteen sister dives into the refrigerator at ten at night and binges on food, explaining that she is just hungry, that is probably defensive. It's defensive because she is not conscious that she is using the good feeling of a full stomach to assuage the hurt feelings of jealousy. Defensiveness is unconscious and it is designed to relieve hurt feelings.

Some of the sexual changes going on in her body are just too sudden, too extreme to bear. It is too hard for her to accept the crazy notion that she would like to have her older sister's boyfriend for herself, and do the things she saw them doing in the car. When the pressure gets too high, feelings that can't be admitted, even to oneself, get rejected, and explanations unconsciously come to mind. Those are the perceptual distortions whose only possible function is to relieve the pressure of growing feelings of sexuality. And the nighttime binges are also aimed at alleviating feelings. That is what a defense is—action taken to feel better and to avoid the reality *causing* the bad feelings.

What is a better way? Talk about it. Don't push for her to admit these internal shifts—she does not even know consciously that she is making them. Just discuss the pressure in a nonthreatening way and leave it there. With time, and with maturation, it may sink in.

Boys' Emotional Development

We have written first about girls' emotional development because girls mature emotionally before boys and because women usually do better with feelings than men. Since women's greater feeling responses have given us a better opportunity to deal with emotions, we shall not repeat what applies to both sexes but shall focus here only on those aspects of boys' emotional and social development that are different and thus require different parenting.

Boys talk proudly about their growing sexual development. The boys will tend to tease each other and compete for faster sexual development. Those who have had wet dreams will often taunt those who have not. Boys arriving at school might boast: "Hey, did I have a wicked wet dream last night! Joey, have you had a wet dream yet? I don't know, kid, you just may never grow up."

Why this different attitude? Most boys are proud of their growing muscular bodies. Boys' genitalia are hidden by pants and do not make a visual public declaration to the world. Girls' growing breasts cannot be as easily hidden, and some girls have a difficult time accepting their change.

It's not all easy sledding for boys, however. The competition increases their sensitivity to failures, mistakes. Many boys desire sexual growth but not all of them are ready for sexual experiences. They are caught in a bind. They want their bodies to become more masculine, but they are not ready for sexual experimentation. Yet they feel the pressure from older boys and some of their peers to get sexual experience. These boys have to make choices, and the choices are difficult. They also feel the demand to perform as athletes, and those with more developed bodies generally do better. That creates a tough situation for the smaller boys who also want to shine.

Sexual fantasies and masturbation are both thrilling and scary. And here again, the male openness about sex among peers leaves little opportunity for privacy and gentle growth. When this male writer was growing up he was assailed with both taunts and encouragement from peers and felt that nothing was private or sacred. How did all those other guys know what I thought happened only to me? I felt invaded!

Then there is the ambivalence, the double bind: Boys get teased if they are interested in girls and if they are not. Is it masculine to like girls or to hate them? Some of the "fast" guys are envied for their prowess with girls; some of the clean-cut types are admired because they scorn girls. How is a boy to know which way to go?

The problem for boys grows as their sexual interest in girls increases: The rules are in transition but still largely demand that the boy make the sexual moves. Usually, he has to do the inviting, which can be extremely difficult. Rejection can shake his self-image to the core; acceptance can scare him into dysfunction. It's not easy.

In addition, as we suggested above, the rules are changing and girls are increasingly free to initiate social and sexual invitations. Some boys are more comfortable with that, others feel overwhelmed. The struggle to gain control and act "manly" is thus not only difficult but demands judgment. Sometimes it is manly to accept the invitation; sometimes it is manly to gently but firmly refuse in some magic way that preserves the girl's dignity along with her virginity. And that can be a wonderful way of showing the way love and appropriate sex can go together. Too much to ask of a preteen boy? Probably not—we have seen it happen many times.

Of course manliness and self control are expected of growing boys in situations other than sex. Social and educational demands are strong. Parents have at once to help and encourage self-help. They make continuous judgment calls which involve giving responsibility and placing limits and controls while teaching and modeling at the same time.

How can parents do it? Essentially by following the same guidelines as for girls: Hang on to your values, make them clear to your son, appreciate your own limited control over his behavior, and don't overreact. In addition, be aware that boys generally do act out more often and more vigorously than girls. Many parents try to handle this with more discipline and toughness. Often that boomerangs because the tight structure you impose substitutes for *consequences* society will impose. For example, if you wake your son every school morning and supervise his dressing, eating, and getting off to school, he will never learn that if he is tardy the school will impose consequences. If, a few years later, you do that so that he won't be late for work, he will never learn that his own failure to be ready on time can cost him his job.

The second reason to be wary of too much control is that your child, and all other normal human beings, direct their anger at the controlling person or institution. Then a power struggle follows. Your son will be angry at you for getting him up and out, and will struggle with you about it. "Why don't you leave me alone, I can always get a ride if I miss the bus." Want to guess who will have to give him that ride?

If you allow him to be late, he becomes aware of the consequences that follow, and he directs his anger at society and the world instead of you. And, he has to work it out with society and the world. Most of the time, society has more power than parents and does a better job of shaping your kid's behavior than you can.

One more point about teaching boys about love and sex. Times are changing and new values are developing in our society. One of them is for male tenderness and feeling. We have learned that men have the capacity to be loving and to understand feelings. We have further learned that both men and women do better in life if men are encouraged to understand and show feelings. We have almost arrived at the point where being sensitive is a manly characteristic which a man can show with pride. So teach your son about feelings. When he inquires about a social situation, ask how he thinks the other person feels about it, how the other person would feel if he did this or that. Get him used to *naming* feelings: anger, respect, hurt, etc. Get him to name what he expects his own feelings would be if he were to take one course of action or another.

Our goal here is to teach boys that *feelings are part of the data that goes into any interpersonal decision.* Boys usually don't realize this. Boys, and men, usually devalue feelings. They state that feelings contaminate decisions: "If you would just be reasonable and look at the logic without all the emotional stuff we could get someplace here." Love and sex are feelings in the purest sense of the word. Girls seem to know that from birth. Boys often need to learn it.

Social Development

Preteens usually burst out in adultlike social activity. They show interest in the opposite sex. There are more parties, more group activities, and the sexes manage to weave each other into their pursuits. Sue may invite Jason over to study—and they may even really study together! And the seemingly opposite also happens: They avoid closeness, avoid touching, get more modest, and avoid nudity.

Both sexes show a growing interest in public communications like advertising, television, video cassette recorders, radios, movies, newspapers, and magazines. From these they learn how sexually maturing people act, and what values they share. They get more interested in music and art, especially as it represents their generation. They are fascinated with the people who populate their world of music, art, and drama. They emulate them and search out their love interests.

The demands are heavy. School is a more serious business and adults are already asking about vocational and career interests. College looms in the far distance. Each sex feels required to define itself: The girls must appear more womanly and the boys more manly. They also want to define themselves as individuals: The boys who can fix cars have a special identity; the girls who become proficient figure skaters know better who they are.

If they fail to meet those social demands, the reaction is intense. They feel themselves rejected by adults and peers alike. The depression is poignant, overwhelming. Perhaps there is only one period of life that is harder, and that is the one coming up, adolescence.

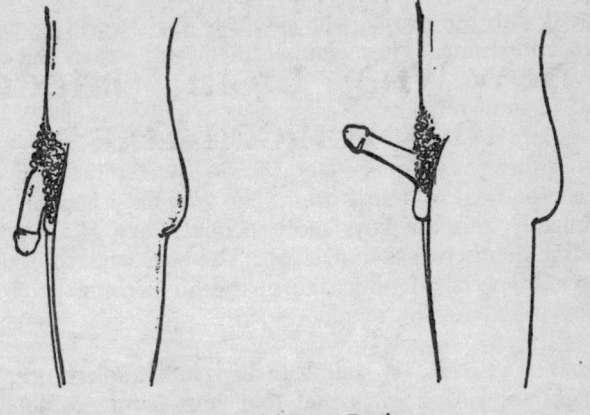

Flaccid and Erect Penis

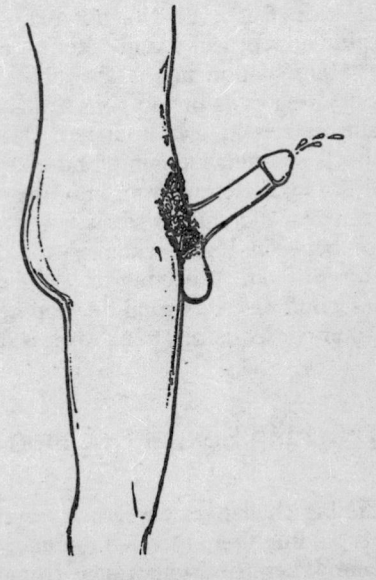

Ejaculation

CHAPTER FIVE

Now What? From Thirteen to Seventeen Years

Once your child is well launched into adolescence, you might think that you could fold your hands, settle down with a well-deserved sigh, and relax. You've told your child basically everything he needs to know. It should be all over and done with. But is it? No, not really. What was once theoretical is now practical and takes on a wholly different meaning. Menstruation in the abstract is one thing. Decisions about using pads or tampons are another. Discussing wet dreams carries its own anxieties. Dealing with semen-stained sheets another. Explaining how babies are conceived and born is a lot different from knowing—or fearing—that your fifteen-year-old child is sexually active. Explaining the difference between heterosexuality and homosexuality is quite different from suspecting or learning that your child is gay. For good *and* ill, sexual development is an ongoing process—and consequently, your work is far from over.

Teaching Sexual Decision-Making

One of the big challenges we face as parents of adolescent children is guiding them through the many sexual decisions facing them. These decisions range from attending school dances to dating to kissing to petting to intercourse. Children grow up faster these days and have to make decisions long before we ever did.

Denise, a beautiful fourteen-year-old, told us solemnly, "I'd never have sex before I'm sixteen. I will certainly remain a virgin until then."

Sally, her best friend, nodded in agreement. "Me, too," she said. "I'd never do it until I was at least sixteen."

Incidentally, they were right. At sixteen each had sex, by seventeen each had had an abortion. There was a reason for this sorry progression. Each girl had parents who panicked as their daughters became more popular and more beautiful. Each set of parents began accusing their respective daughters of being "sluts" or "whores," and the girls responded accordingly. Both Sally and Denise told us that they'd learned about sex and contraception through friends. Each knew about the Pill and got it, then decided pregnancy wouldn't happen to her—but it did. It is important to note that neither girl had any pride in herself. Each had been totally demoralized by her parents' accusations. At no time did the girls feel that they had the support and sympathy of their parents.

Michael's mother came in red-faced and red-eyed. She had repeatedly told her son that she would never tolerate abortion. She kept warning him—he was fourteen when she began—that if he got a girl pregnant, he'd have to marry her. When he was fifteen, he impregnated a girl of sixteen. Both sets of parents agreed abortion was the only possible solution and saw that it was carried out. Michael kept twitting his mother, saying, "I thought you didn't approve of abortion. What's with you?"

What is much more effective and much more pleasant for both parent and child is for you, the parents, to continue to enhance your children's self-esteem by reinforcing their good judgment and continuing to remind them, just as you did when they were little, that their bodies are wonderful and are worthy of respect and care. That also means that, as parents, you have to provide your children with information about sexual safety, as well as exploring with them what friendship means and what love involves. Implicit in that is the respect you have for your children ... or else you wouldn't be talking with them. You'd be yelling or threatening, as did the parents of Sally, Denise, and Michael.

It is interesting to note that we've had many conversations with young women in their twenties and thirties who say basically the same thing—"No, no one ever told me about sex." When we say in reply, "Well, what about school?" they say, "Oh, that? Yeah. A little." When we press on and ask, "Well, didn't your mother tell you about menstruation?" the answer is, "Oh, yeah. She did that, but that's not about sex." These women all looked sad when they talked about their lack of communication with their parents about these intimate matters. These young women seemed to feel that not only did they have to seek out information by themselves, but they also had to formulate values without any real guidance from their parents. We feel strongly that it's important to stay in close touch with your adolescents not only to provide them with information but also to guide them through the delicate choices that they have to make during these important years.

Specifically what kind of information are we talking about? Information about responsibility is primary. Children should know that it is their responsibility to select a girlfriend or boyfriend who is kind, dependable, wholesome, and thoughtful, someone who can make careful choices and respect another person's choices. And both boys and girls should know how to protect themselves from unwanted pregnancies. They should know that abortion is never synonymous with birth control. They should know how to protect themselves from sexually transmitted diseases, and they should know what measures they can take to prevent rape. It's a tall order but a vital one. Children deserve and value the information and, even more important, the sharing with parents. Not that they make it easy for us:

"Can't you see I'm busy?"
"Do we have to talk about that now?"

"Not that again!"
"Tom's gonna call in four minutes. I gotta go."

If you hang in, however, you notice that they come back when they're ready (maybe one or two hours later) and give you the supreme privilege of talking. "Well, here I am, whaddya want now?" It's almost as if they need to impose some sort of control on us—and that's okay. That's part of the challenge of adolescence: figuring out where the new boundaries are, where it's safe to give in, where it's safe to disagree and demand. Your challenge as parents is to be patient and wait. Of course, a sense of humor helps. It also helps to remind yourself that this is the time when your children are making increasingly more difficult decisions: Who knows more, themselves, the gang, or their parents? How will the gang feel about me if I'm different? Is it worth it? It's a tough time for parents—and it's also a tough time for our kids.

For example, it's safe to assume that if your child has not yet made a choice to be sexually active, sooner or later he will make such a decision. It would make your job as parents easier if children would postpone sex until marriage. And a few will. But most won't, regardless of your own regard for virginity and your religion's regard for chastity. Whatever children choose, however, they deserve to have the information they need in order to make responsible choices.

At this point, we think it is important to make certain assumptions: One is that your children are aware of what your opinion is about sexual relationships at an early age and without marriage. If asked, we're sure that 98 percent of all children would report their parent's feelings accurately. That being the case, it makes no sense to *demand* that your child not have sex. You should state your preference about his embarking on a sexual adventure. He needs to be absolutely clear about your opinion. But it is useless to insist that your child not have sex or try to punish him or scold him if you disapprove of his decision to be sexually active. If he's made his decision to have intercourse—with or without your approval—then the least we can do is to see to it that he continues with safety and responsibility.

So how would we begin? We'd start something like this:

Mother:	You know, Samantha, Dad and I get a great kick out of seeing how much you enjoy being with Scott. There's nothing better than love. *[At this point, we're going to assume that you and your partner are living together. If not, you can always reminisce about how you once did love, or wish that you had.]*
Samantha:	Yeah. So?
Mother:	And it's fun to kiss and hug. And it's exciting to touch and be touched.
Samantha:	Mother!
Mother:	And when you really love someone and then are married to him, there's no more wonderful expression of love than sex.
Samantha:	Mom! Really!
Mother:	Samantha, I hope you're not embarrassed by this. I was never able to talk to your grandmother about any of this and always wished I could. I had to make a lot of decisions and it was hard. I want you to know I love you and respect you and want to be there for you.
Samantha:	Listen, Mom, this is sort of weird.
Mother:	That's okay. It's a little weird for me, too. But there's a lot I want to tell you.
Samantha:	I don't know about this—
Mother:	When I was in high school I wanted to be popular. I wanted to go to the dances. But I didn't know whether I should kiss my date or pet with him, or even have sex. I couldn't talk to Grandma about it. My friends said, "Do it." But that didn't help. It was a hard time.
Samantha:	Well, what did you do?

Mother: I finally decided it was all right to hold hands and to kiss, if you liked the guy. And maybe petting if you really liked him.

Samantha: Good grief!

Mother: Yeah, I know. But by college most of my friends were having intercourse with the guys they loved and most of them married them.

Samantha: What did you do?

Mother: I waited for your father and marriage.

Samantha: Good girl. How about Dad?

Mother: He had several love affairs before we met.

Samantha: He told you?

Mother: Oh, sure.

Samantha: So Dad had been around.

Mother: Yes. But he had loved these women, or so he said. That makes a difference.

Samantha: Why?

Mother: Well, to me it means that he cared about them. He didn't just use them. He was faithful to them while he was with them. Just as he has been with me.

Samantha: That's great.

Mother: I'm glad you agree. I think so, too. But I've told you about me. And what I said is between us, okay? Now, what about you?

Samantha: What about me?

Mother: Well, we don't know much about Scott. We know how you light up but we don't really know what he's like.

Samantha: What do you mean?

Mother: Well, your father and I feel very strongly that men should treat women as well as they treat men. And vice versa. You know, be someone you can count on. Someone who keeps his word. Someone who respects you and your feelings. Someone who is concerned about your having a good time as well as him. Do you know what I mean?

Samantha:	Not really. Just what are you talking about? Scott would never hurt me. He's my friend.
Mother:	Well, I'm delighted to hear that. But if something should happen to this relationship, we hope that you would always insist that your man would treat you respectfully, be dependable, and be kind.
Samantha:	Look, Mom, don't worry. I know what I'm doing.
Mother:	Dad and I think you're pretty level-headed. We just know how easy it is to get talked into things before you're ready. Like sex.
Samantha:	Look, Mom, that's my business. Cool it!
Mother:	For now. But let's talk later. There's a lot more to say.
Samantha:	Well, maybe. Sure. Later.

We hope in this dialogue to share our concern that children make their own decision about sex or any aspect of it because it seems right to them, not because of peer pressure or for the need to be popular. We would also want your children to pick a partner who is decent, kind, respectful, and responsible. Just the kinds of qualities we would hope they would bring to any relationship.

This dialogue, with its particular goals, is applicable to boys as well as to girls. Although it was a mother talking to her daughter, it could just as well be a mother talking to her son or a father talking to his daughter or son. As we've said, it doesn't matter which parent does the talking. What *does* matter is that the talk is held.

In this dialogue, the mother was quite candid about her past. Is it necessary? You can only do what you are comfortable with. If you can share, it might bring you and your child closer. It's also all right to say, "I'm not comfortable sharing that part of my life with you. It's always been a private part of my life. Maybe later I can tell you more, but not now." Your child can certainly understand that. There's a lot our children elect not to share with us.

And there's a lot to discuss with our adolescents. Can it all be done in one conversation? No. We find that children get restless. Then, if we push on, we sound as if we're delivering a sermon from the pulpit. Then there is a terrible silence. It's all been said. End of intimacy. Naturally, if your child wants to continue or ask questions, you would continue, if you have the time. You have rights, too. But, ideally, you would try to make time for these conversations. When children have a need to know, they are relatively indifferent to our inconvenience. But we've known that for years.

Talking About Contraception

Contraception for our children is a big issue for most of us to handle. However liberated we may feel, when the time comes to talk to our young ones, it's hard. It's never easy to acknowledge our child's sexuality. There's a lot of comfort in thinking that what you don't know won't hurt you: "I figured it out. They can, too. They'll learn it in school. Their friends will tell them. They probably know all about it anyway. If I tell them, they'll think they can go out and be promiscuous." A lot of parents tell us they worry about that. They fear that if they talk to their children about methods of birth control, it is tantamount to giving them permission to run out and have sex. But your children know your values. They know how you feel about adolescent sex and premarital sex. Values aren't vaccinations that you give to your child in one shot. They are an ongoing concern. And, of course, you would preface your explanation with a statement again about your values. What you are providing is information, not permission: that you do prefer that sex occur after marriage—if indeed that is the way you feel. No matter what the values, however, you want your child to be informed and prepared for any eventuality.

Now, your child may know about contraception, but he

may not know how you feel about it. In addition, he may not know where to go for contraceptive materials. There is also the kind of bravado that insulates many young people— "Oh, just this once. It will never happen to me. I don't need that stuff." Your child needs to know that it can happen just that one time and that an ovum can be fertilized even without intercourse. He also needs to know the advantages and disadvantages of the various methods of contraception. Does this mean that you have to be an authority on all the various ways of preventing birth? Well, you can be. Planned Parenthood has excellent material available. Some of the books we list in our Bibliography do, too. You can refer your child to some books for information, but you must also explore the subject with your child, because it is your guidance and interest and concern that will help him make responsible choices when the time comes.

Teaching About Sexually Transmitted Diseases and Abortion

You want your children to know two primary things: should they elect to become sexually active with a partner, they both need to prevent pregnancy and disease. All this comes under the headings of respect for self and others, and good health.

How would you go about this? Again, we'd suggest you find a time when you can be alone, preferably without interruption from the telephone. You know teenagers. The telephone is their lifeline and takes precedence over anything else. And once you're interrupted, it's hard to get back to where you want to be. So, short of cutting your telephone line, you might try a walk together, or a drive together, or even a restaurant where you can be guaranteed some privacy. You might try something like this:

Mother: Samantha, you remember when we talked about relationships with guys, and being kind and insisting that they be kind to you? Well, today I'd like to discuss contraception with you.

Samantha: Oh, Mom, I know all about it.

Mother: Well, maybe you do, but perhaps you don't know exactly how Dad and I feel about it. I'd like to share some thoughts with you and maybe some information that you don't have.

Samantha: Scott is going to be calling me. I have to get back. Will this take long?

Mother: Don't know. As long as we need. But we'll both remember that Scott is going to call.

Samantha: All right. Now what?

Mother: Look. This is kind of tough for me. I always knew I would want you to know about contraception. It's hard to get going. To begin with, just because I'm talking to you about it doesn't mean that Dad and I are giving you permission to go out and have sex. Actually, neither Dad nor I approve of sex before marriage. But we also know people can get carried away. Whatever your decision, we want you to be responsible about it. That means protecting yourself from pregnancy or any form of sexually transmitted diseases.

Samantha: Listen, Mom, if you're talking about AIDS, I know all about it. The school nurse talked to us. You just make sure the boy uses condoms.

Mother: No, honey, I'm talking about more than that. I'm talking about feeling good enough about yourself so that you can refuse if you don't want to do anything that is not right for you. You've probably heard that if a boy gets very excited and he has to stop, he'll go crazy or get very painful testicles. Well, he won't go crazy, and the pain will go away. You always have the right to say no. Don't ever forget that.

Samantha: You've told me that before. I know that.

Mother: Good. But you need to know more. Did you know that you can get pregnant without intercourse?

Samantha: Mom! What are you talking about?

Mother: Well, all you need is a strong sperm to be near the vagina and then start to swim up to meet an ovum, and you have a baby on the way. Just petting can be serious.

Samantha: Has that ever happened, really?

Mother: Yes. I know two women who had virgin births, as it were. Each insisted that she didn't have intercourse and got pregnant and then married. They were very bitter.

Samantha: Wow! Who are they?

Mother: I won't tell you. It wouldn't be fair. I made a promise to them. But I want you to know that it does happen.

Samantha: Oh, God, I'd die if that happened to me.

Mother: Well, that's why I'm telling you. Dad and I want you alive.

Samantha: Geez! What else?

Mother: Well, Dad and I want you to be responsible should you ever decide to have sex with someone. And that means birth control.

Samantha: Yeah, yeah. You said that, and I know all about it. I think Scott will be calling soon.

Mother: What would you do if you decided to try alcohol, or pot, then got carried away and had sex?

Samantha: Hey, Mom, I wouldn't do that. What do you take me for?

Mother: Well, I'm glad to hear that. But what would you do?

Samantha: I suppose this is your way to tell me not to do drugs or drink?

Mother: Since both are illegal, I would hope you wouldn't. But just what would you do to be safe?

Samantha: How do I know? God, Mom. I've really got to get going.

Mother: Well, that's why I'm talking with you. You have to think. If you are going to be sexually active, you ought to consider the Pill. That provides the most protection against pregnancy. It means that you take a pill daily for three weeks and then stop for a week. A doctor has to prescribe it. That means a pelvic examination first. If the idea of taking chemicals doesn't appeal to you, there are other choices, such as inserting vaginal foams, or jellies or sponges, into the vagina just before intercourse. Some find that pretty inconvenient. Then there is the diaphragm, which is a kind of rubber cap that fits over the cervix and prevents sperm from entering. It must be fitted by a physician. It is fairly simple to insert but, again, requires a bit of planning ahead if you're going to use it safely. And it must be used with a foam or jelly. With diaphragms, and foams and jellies and sponges, it is better if a man uses a condom. That way there is much more protection. The pill is the safest and the most convenient. However, it will not protect you against any sexually transmitted diseases. It does offer the best protection against pregnancy. But in terms of sexually transmitted diseases, a condom is necessary.

Samantha: Well, are you saying that a condom is the best way?

Mother: Of course it's not a 100 percent guarantee against either pregnancy or diseases. Used in combination with a woman's using a vaginal sponge or foam or diaphragm, it can be pretty effective. A condom has to be used with a jelly. You see, without it, the condom would be irritating to the tender tissues of your vagina. You would need the lubrication that the jelly provides. At the moment, condoms provide the best protection against sexually transmitted diseases.

Samantha: Then why do boys hate them?

Mother: Well, it does mean interrupting one's sexual excitement to put one on. It's kind of clumsy, but a lot better than getting herpes, you know.

Samantha: Mom, this is kind of yucky.

Mother: So is having a baby at fifteen, or finding yourself with herpes. Look, sex is a wonderful, exciting experience. But it also means lots of responsibility and decisions. But I can see you're getting restless. Tell you what. Suppose I get some books on the subject of contraception and we'll read them and decide what looks right. Mind you, I'm not suggesting you do have intercourse. Dad and I feel strongly that you ought to be prepared, then think through what you're doing, and be responsible for your choice. We also want you to feel free to talk to us at any time. And listen. This wasn't so bad. You're a good kid. We love you."

Samantha: You're okay, Mom. But, Mom, where do I go to get any of this stuff?

Mother: Well, condoms, foams, jellies, and sponges are for sale at any drugstore. You don't need a prescription for any of them. You do need to make an appointment with a doctor for either the Pill or the diaphragm. That means a pelvic examination to make sure that you are okay for the pill, or that the diaphragm fits your cervical opening properly.

Samantha: Well, what about abortion? That sounds easier than any of this other stuff.

Mother: I'm glad you raised that. I was going to talk to you about it. Do you know what abortion means?

Samantha: Yes, sort of. It means scraping the fetus out, doesn't it?

Mother: Yes, that's about it. But it also means a medical procedure, followed by cramps and bleeding, and the knowledge that you have stopped a life. It's a very serious business. It's not a method of birth control. Control means think first, then act. Abortion is after the fact. And it's ugly.

Samantha: Mom, did you ever have an abortion?

Mother: No, thank goodness. But I know some women who have, and they have never gotten over it. You know, it's easy to say that you shouldn't be ashamed or feel guilty, but they do. It even gets in the way of relationships with men. It's almost as though women get to feeling unworthy and can't speak up for themselves.

Samantha: Well, Mom, if you feel that way, how come you support legal abortion?

Mother: Oh, I'm glad you asked. Let's get some things straight. There is such a thing as a therapeutic abortion. It is the same process but for a different reason. Suppose a woman finds she has a serious disease, such as cancer, and discovers she is pregnant, or suppose a woman is raped and then finds she is pregnant. Maybe a girl is impregnated by her father or brother, or finds out during the pregnancy that she's been exposed to German measles and finds that the baby will be hideously deformed. Those are, to me, valid reasons for abortion. But abortion is not for birth control. Contraception is. Got it?

Samantha: Got it. But why do girls have to do everything? It's not fair. We have to make the choice of contraception, abortion, everything. I'd rather be a boy. They have it easy.

Mother: That thought has crossed my mind more than once. On the other hand, look at it this way, they never experience the thrill of giving birth.

Samantha: That doesn't cut it with me. Boys don't even menstruate.

Mother: True. But they have erections when they don't want them, and that's pretty embarrassing, I guess.

Samantha: Phooey!

Mother: Yeah, I know. But that's why Dad and I want you to be very aware of choices and the seriousness of some of the decisions you will be making. You do have a lot of responsibility for yourself. All girls do. And that's the way it is.

Samantha: Mom, I think you're pretty cool. Like, excellent.

Mother: Wow! Thanks.

Samantha: But, Mom, what would you do if I did get pregnant?

Mother: Look, the reason I just explained contraception to you was so that you wouldn't need an abortion.

Samantha: Yeah, but what if I did? What would you do?

Mother: Do you mean if it weren't rape or something like that?

Samantha: Yes. What would you do?

Mother: Well, it's not what *I*'d do. It's really what you would have to decide to do. That's why Dad and I want you to be careful. You see, you do have choices, and none of them are easy. You could have the baby and keep it, hoping that your man would stay with you and help you. You could have the baby and put it up for adoption. Or you could decide to abort. Can you see yourself at fourteen as a full-time mother taking care of a child? You'd have to give up school and, with luck, continue at night. It would be the end of all your fun. Babies require lots of care. You know what it was like when Rover was a puppy. Well, babies are ten times worse than that. If you decided to give up the baby, how would you feel about yourself? Would you miss your child when you are older?

Samantha: So it looks as if my choice would be abortion.

Mother: As I said, that's not an easy choice. Then you have to know that you stopped a life. Probably it's better to think about your own life and make sure that it goes as smoothly as you can possibly make it. You are in charge of your body. The best thing is to make sure you use it wisely. Got it?

Samantha: Do other mothers talk to their kids this way?

Mother: I don't know. I told you I wish Grandma and I had been able to.

Samantha: Yeah.

Mother: Look, this has been heavy. There's been a lot to think about. This isn't the only time we can talk about it. Both Dad and I are available for questions and discussions any time. Okay?

Samantha: Okay.

Please note: These are *our* values. Each of you must present your own. For example, if abortion is abhorrent to you, then you will tell your child so, saying that any form of human life is sacred and must be preserved, that for you abortion is tantamount to murder. You'll hope your children will share your convictions but you must realize that *they* are resposible for their choices.

* * *

We'd like to make a few points more about this dialogue. First, we've provided Samantha with information about contraception. Second, her mother has left the door open for further talking and left herself available for questions and talk. Third, the mother has made her value system clear, but left her daughter with the responsibility for making her own choices. And fourth, and most important, the mother has made it plain that if Samantha gets pregnant, she is the one who will live with it. The parents are there to be helpful but are not going to die or collapse or throw her out if she does get in trouble.

This last point is very important. So many of the young girls and boys with whom we work get into a power struggle with their parents. These are the parents who have hurled insults at them. These are the parents who make an ugly issue of getting pregnant. These are the parents who make a dirty deal out of abortions. And these actions are like hurling a red flag in front of a bull. The next step is almost inevitable. The boy whose mother insists that she could never tolerate abortions impregnates his girlfriend at the age of fourteen and then watches Mother swallow her words as she pleads with the girl to have an abortion. As soon as a parent says that an abortion would kill her, her daughter is pregnant. She may not tell Mom, but she does have an abortion.

Does this mean that our kids are mean and vindictive? No. But it does mean that adolescence is a time of testing limits, of finding out just how serious parents are when they utter their threats. So it is far more effective to place the responsibilty for their sexual decisions squarely on the shoulders of our children. We must provide information. We must supply our value systems. We must make sure they know they have our love and support. We must avoid hypocrisy. But we mustn't allow our children to manipulate us with rash actions.

We have been using a lot of mother/daughter dialogues,

but that does not mean that just daughters have problems. Boys, as we have said, need to know from their parents about responsibility and sex just as much as girls do. In a way, they are perhaps even more victimized by stereotypical thinking than are girls. Think of all they have to live up to—boys are macho, boys know everything, boys are always interested in just one thing, SEX!, and so on. In fact, boys are just as puzzled and confused as girls, just as much in need of information and a place to explore. As a matter of fact, boys are human beings. At fourteen, boys do not automatically turn into some sort of sex maven or maniac. At fourteen, what they are is boys who are trying to figure out what growing up is all about.

We would certainly, therefore, tell them about the responsibilities of sex in terms of love and kindness, of safety and of preventing pregnancy. And we would do it in the following way. Again, it doesn't matter if Mom or Dad does the talking. If they can do it together, so much the better.

Father:	I notice that when the phone rings these days it's usually for you and it's usually a girl.
Son:	Yeah, so?
Father:	Well, we think it's great that people like you and are calling you. How do you feel about it?
Son:	It's okay. This isn't a big deal.
Father:	Hmm. What we think is a big deal is the way people treat each other.
Son:	What are you talking about?
Father:	Well, sometimes people seem to think that when you're kind of trying to decide which boy or girl you like, the regular rules for friendship don't apply.
Son:	I don't get it. What do you mean?
Father:	Oh, you know, handing a girl a line. Telling her how much you like her when, in fact, you don't. You'd never do that to another guy. Why treat a girl any differently? As a matter of fact, leading someone on is mean. It's not kind. We hope you'd be honest with any girl.

Son: It's all part of the fun. They do it to us.

Father: Sounds like a game where feelings can be really hurt. As I said, it's a mean game with no winners."

Son: Well, I'll think about it.

Father: Good. That's fine. You know, when I was your age I thought that I was supposed to know everything about love and sex and take the lead. I never really knew what I was supposed to do, and it was pretty scary. I had no older brothers to talk to. It sure was confusing. It never occurred to me I could talk to my father. It was a hard time. But I did learn to treat girls fairly—because that's how I wanted them to treat me.

Son: Did they?

Father: Yeah, for the most part. Pretty much if I was honest with them, they were honest with me. Anyway, I felt better about myself and had more respect for myself.

We'd leave the subject there. As parents, we sometimes pound points home, insisting that our children agree with us absolutely. In fact, they rarely do to our faces. But a lot of thinking goes on. They have to think it through in such a way that the idea is theirs, and then it's okay.

But we would continue the conversation at another time because we would want our sons to know about responsibility for their sexual safety and for preventing unwanted pregnancy. We would suggest that you begin with a discussion of your values. As we pointed out earlier, this is the time when you have to face up to your values about sex—specifically, whether you feel boys should be "macho" and try sex as soon as possible or should be more conservative. We're going to assume that you would prefer your sons to be more conservative before they experiment with sex. Of course, you must supply your own values. There is no point in pretending, either. Children have an uncanny ability to detect phoniness immediately.

Father: You know, Al, we were talking about treating girls kindly the other day.

Son: Not that again!

Father: No. I want to go on to something else. We've explained to you how babies are conceived. Well, now I want to tell you how babies are *not* conceived.

Son: What? What do you mean?

Father: Well, of course, the best way not to have a baby is not to have sex. But there are ways of preventing birth if you do have sex. I would like you to know about them. That doesn't mean that Mom and I [or Dad and I] want you to experiment. That's part of what we meant when we talked about treating girls kindly— and insisting that they treat you kindly. And because we are talking about methods of contraception, that doesn't mean that we are giving you our permission to go out and have sex. Understand? We're giving you information so that you can make responsible choices.

Son: Listen, Dad, if you're talking about condoms, I know all about them.

Father: Do you? Good. That's part of what I wanted to talk to you about, but it's not the whole story. Of course, if you use a condom, the chances are that your girl won't get pregnant. They're pretty good if you use them right. And, of course, girls can control pregnancy, too.

Son: You mean the Pill? I know all about that, too.

Father: Oh, great! I'm glad you're so well informed. Girls didn't have the Pill in my day. But we boys did have condoms. It was sort of a big deal to always carry them in our wallets. Showed we were really cool.

Son: Where did you get them?

Father: In the drugstore. Just like today.

Son: Did Grampa know you had them?

Father: Never! You just didn't discuss this with your parents when I was a kid.

Son: Why didn't you talk to Grandpa?

Father: Well, now that I think about it, I don't know. Sex was just a big secret in those days. What I knew I learned from the guys who had older brothers. I vowed I would talk to my kid, if I was lucky enough to have one.

Son: Well, look, Dad, I guess I know everything. I know about AIDS and condoms. We talk about it in Health. I know how to prevent pregnancy. Anyway, it's up to the girl to take care of herself. Like you said, she's got the Pill. It's not my problem.

Father: Wrong! It *is* your problem. That's one of the reasons I was talking to you about being kind to a girl. And picking a girl who is kind to you.

Son: I don't get it.

Father: Well, suppose you did get a girl pregnant. You are equally responsible for the life of that baby. Should the girl elect to keep the baby, then you're financially responsible for that child until the child is eighteen years old. Can you see yourself supporting a family at your age? That would be the end of your football, for sure.

Son: Oh, come on! Everybody knows about abortion. She could have one of those.

Father: Yes, she could. If you both so chose. But remember, you are part of the process. And that means that if you did decide to stop the birth, you would have participated in stopping a life. And that's serious business. You would also be responsible for at least part payment for the abortion. So that's a lot to think about. You have three choices: fatherhood, terminating life, or responsibility and precaution.

Son: Well, don't worry about it.

Father: I won't. You're the one who has to live with the consequences. I'll feel bad if you get into any trouble, but you're the one who'll live with whatever happens. It's like sexually transmitted diseases. You can take chances. But you're the one who lives with the results. Remember that. That's why we urge you to treat girls with respect. And make sure they are worthy of respect. Got it?

Son: Listen, I gotta go now. See you later.

Father: Fine. I'll give you a slogan to take with you—it's your body and your life.

Son: All right, all right. See you later.

More on Sexually Transmitted Diseases, and AIDS

So far, we've been talking about parenting your child, exploring with your child your values about love and sex, and cautioning him about his responsibility. Unfortunately, you also need to explain to your children some of the hazards of sex. It seems unreasonable that such a pleasant, natural process can also be a source of danger. But it is so, and children must know that. We refer, of course, to sexually transmitted diseases (STDs). Specifically, we mean venereal diseases, such as gonorrhea, syphilis, herpes, and the worst, AIDS. What your children should know is that gonorrhea and syphilis, if treated in time, can be cured. There is no cure for herpes.

All of the aforementioned diseases are sexually transmitted. That means you get them from having sex with an infected partner. And Acquired Immune Deficiency Syndrome, or AIDS, is fatal. There is no cure for it. AIDS can be acquired from infected partners, blood transfusions, exchanging dirty needles, or allowing infected blood to come into contact with an open wound.

Does this mean that you now have to become an expert on STDs as part of your parenting? Once again, we suggest that you have some books on hand that explore STDs in greater depth than we have here. We list some in our bibliography. But it is helpful to have a quick source to refer to when you are talking with your adolescent. Nowhere is it written that parents have to know *everything*, but knowing what your children are talking about and likely thinking about and having source material at hand is a great help. The papers and TV are now so filled with articles about AIDS that it makes exploring the whole topic of STDs much easier and logical.

A natural way to lead into such a discussion is to pick up an article in the newspaper or plan to watch a program about AIDS on TV with your child. Armed with your material on STDs, you have a wonderful opportunity to explain to your child what it is he needs to know. It's a temptation to wait for the school to take care of this one, but your child may have questions that he is embarrassed to ask in front of a whole class. And can you be sure that that was the day he was paying strict attention or, for that matter, even in class?

If you have used a newspaper article or watched TV, we'd follow up like this:

Parent: It seems you can't be too careful about picking a partner.

Child: Don't worry about it.

Parent: Will you worry about it so that you will be super-careful about the people you go with?

Child: Don't make a case out of it.

Parent: Well, it's true you can live with herpes, although you will be pretty uncomfortable at times. But you can't live with AIDS. And it's a gruesome disease. Condoms are supposed to be pretty effective. At least, that's all they've got right now. Anyone would be out of his mind not to use a condom these days. I think girls should carry them, too. Just in case. You can live through pregnancy. But, AIDS—that's a bad one. Do your friends talk about it at all?

Child: Yeah, we all do. We don't want to die.

Parent: Well, for sure I don't want you to, nor does your mother. But we don't want you to get other diseases, either. One of the best ways to prevent any STD is to be careful and very selective about your partner.

Single Parents Only

Now suppose that mother and father are divorced and living single lives, with a fair amount of dating and inviting partners to sleep over. Suppose your child wants to know at this point what you are doing to be safe? What do you say? To us, it seems like a perfect opportunity to level with your child:

Father: You know, your Mom and I couldn't get along and so we divorced. But that was before AIDS, and so I dated a lot. You know that. You've met a lot of them. Your mother has dated, too. Some of the women I dated I liked a lot. You remember Selma? I thought she was pretty special, and I did make love with her. Actually, I made love with a few others as well. But you suspected that. Now I'm very careful about whom I date. I even ask what her history is. I ask her if she has been with many men, and what kind of men they have been. And I see women are asking me the same kind of questions. They're being very careful, too. It's sure a new world out there. These days it's a lot easier being married and having just one partner. Then you can be sure your partner shares your values.

Child: And what if she doesn't? Bye-bye, lady?

Father: I can't take chances anymore. And neither can you.

Child: What about Mom? Do you think she's being careful?

Father: We talked about it once. But I can't speak for her. Ask her yourself. She won't mind.

Children of single parents are very aware of their parent's dating life. We've never met a kid yet who didn't know that in the morning Sam or Tom or Gloria or Sally would be on the couch but, during the night when the child got up for a glass of water, the date was nowhere to be seen and the bedroom door was firmly shut. It's silly to pretend that nothing is happening. The dilemma for most parents comes when the child says,

"Hey, you're sleeping with others and you're not married to them. Why can't I? What's the big deal? How come I'm supposed to wait until I am older or even married and you're not?"

Those are tough questions and are usually asked by angry children. Again, we would be absolutely up front with our children. Never attempt to deny what they know to be true. But we would explore responsibility, judgment, and even privilege.

"Look, I'm a lot older than you. I can legally drive. I can legally drink. I can vote. I don't have to go to school. Why do you suppose the laws are constructed that way? It has to do with judgment. The law supposes that adults can make good decisions and be responsible for them. So we have more privileges than you do. I can take care of myself in ways that you can't. For instance, I have a job and money. That means I can afford to pay for any consequences that may happen. But what is more important is that I'm careful about whom I am with. I pick my women carefully and like them. I'm not ready to get married yet. It may be a long time before I am, but I will continue to try to find a woman whom I can truly love. Because I can tell you from experience, there's nothing like being with someone with whom you're truly in love and who truly loves you. That's paradise. And don't forget it!"

And if your child continues to challenge you, "Well, what if I do try sex?" try something like, "Your mother and I wish you would wait. But if you won't, be careful. Remember what we told you about picking a partner, and remember what we told you about contraception. I can't control what you do, and neither can your mother. You're in charge."

Notice that in this conversation you're still in control. You have let your child know what your values are, what you would like. And you have let him know that he must take responsibility for his choice. He can't panic you.

Talking About Sexual Abuse

As you remember, one of the ways you have shown your love for your children has been to teach them how to protect themselves from sexual abuse. This began when they were three, and you have continued repeating your warnings and expanding their information. By this age, it shouldn't be necessary to warn again about incest. But in this age of multiple families, and multiple marriages, perhaps it is. Stepparents don't have the incest taboos that parents do. So again, it is wise to tell your children again that they have lovely bodies, that they are in charge of them, and that no one should ask to be allowed to touch any part of their bodies in a way that makes them uncomfortable. Nor should anyone ask them to touch any part of another person's body that makes your child feel uncomfortable.

Should incest or abuse happen, your children must hear that they are not to blame—ever! And you, the parent, must be the one to comfort and reassure your child. Congratulate him for telling you. Reassure him that he did nothing wrong, that you love him and are proud of him for reporting. Naturally, that means you take appropriate action against the perpetrator by reporting to the police, the courts, or your local Department of Social Services. If you see that your child is acting worried or depressed, or is unable to focus, then we recommend counseling for him. The most effective therapy is group therapy where he can meet others, know that he is not alone, and that others have come through such an experience intact. With your support and comfort, he should be okay. Incest is a horrible act, not only for the victim but for the whole family, since disclosure generally means the possible breakup of the family. It would probably be wise for the whole family to get into therapy, also. There are many issues to explore with a sensitive counselor.

Remember, your child may feel that he can't talk to you.

Should he be attacked and not feel he can tell you, direct him to his doctor, grandparents—anyone he trusts who will take action. Usually, schools have nurses and counselors who do a good job at protecting children. But children must be coached to talk to someone who will take action on their behalf.

Talking About Homosexuality

Homosexuality is another area to explore. Our children use words like "fag" rather indiscriminately—derisively but not necessarily accurately. When you hear them use it, however, you might seize that time to explain homosexuality to your child. It's also a good opportunity to explain that homosexuals are people, too.

Parent: You know, I hear you calling your friends fags when you are angry with them. Do you know what the word means?

Child: What do you mean?

Parent: Well, fag is an unkind way to refer to a homosexual. Did you know that?

Child: What's a homosexual? Is that like a homo?

Parent: "Homo" is short for "homosexual." It means that two people of the same sex prefer to be together sexually. In other words, men who prefer to make love with men, and women with women.

Child: How do they do that?

Parent: Well, they can hug and kiss and touch each other's genitals—you know, masturbate each other.

Child: Gross!

Parent: It doesn't appeal to me, either, but the point is that they are human beings also. As a matter of fact, many of them are extremely talented people. Some of them are great athletes. They just have different sex needs.

Child: Al said a man tried to get him.

Parent: That's what we told you about. Remember? We have always told you never to let *anyone*—man or woman—do anything to you that you didn't want done.

Child: Nah, I wouldn't.

Parent: Good. But some people are bisexual. That means they can have sex with either men or women. If a man has sex by putting his penis into someone else's anus, he could get AIDS and then transmit AIDS to his girlfriends.

Child: Yuck! Nobody would do a thing like that. That's disgusting!

Parent: To us, yes. To others, no. In any event, that's why you have to be careful about your partner. Suppose you select a partner who has made love with a bisexual who had made love to a homosexual who might have AIDS? It gets very complicated and very dangerous. That's why you really do have to be careful to pick someone to love very carefully. Sorry, kid. But that's life.

Talking About Rape

We have been exploring ways to protect our children sexually. One last bit of information remains—rape. We handle rape much the same way we have been treating incest or other forms of sexual molestation. We would provide ways of preventing rape, ways of protecting against it, and ways of protesting against it. In addition to exploring protection with daughters, you should certainly discuss it with your sons in terms of respecting a woman and treating her appropriately. "Date rape" is all-too common.

Since there is at least one case of rape reported almost daily in our newspapers, a newspaper article is a good way to start the discussion with our young teenager. This doesn't have to be a private conversation. All the children in the family from the age of seven on can benefit. And if both parents can be present, so much the better. To begin with, we'd define rape as forcing a man or woman to have sexual intercourse against his or her will. It's an ugly thing to do to another human being. It's painful and humiliating and awful. It's a crime, punishable by law. And we'd go on to remind our children that making love should be a loving act, one that both parties would agree to, not be forced to do. Then we'd remind them of our warnings of the past.

Parent: Do you remember how we used to tell you never to accept bribes from strangers? Do you remember how we used to tell you that you had the right never to let anyone touch you in your private parts? Well, rape is different in that once you're in the middle of it, there may be little you can do except concentrate on living. If he has a gun or knife or some other weapon, there isn't much you can do to protect yourself. But do you know what you can do to prevent it?

Child: You mean, like not going with strangers?

Parent: Yup. That's good. And how about walking alone down dark streets?

Child: Well, sometimes you can't help it.

Parent: Hmm. Well then, try to walk near the curb so that you can run, and always scream loudly so that someone might hear you and call the police.

Child: I'd die if I were raped.

Parent: There's no reason to. There's a lot you can do to prevent it. But remember, it isn't your fault, no matter how it happens. You have a right to be safe. We would always love you and support you. And we'd help you make good choices about getting help. We'd be absolutely furious with anyone who tried to hurt you but we want you any way we can get you. And that's why we are talking about this now.

Child: What if I went off with someone you told me not to, and he hurt me?

Parent: Hey, remember what I've told you, and your mother, too. It's your body. We want you to keep it safe and healthy. So you have to make good choices about whom you go with. Make sure you know him and know something about him. And make sure he doesn't take you out on a lonely road. And let's talk about what you would do if someone tries to force you to go with him from a party. What would you do?

Child: Well, I could yell.

Parent: Good. And sit down fast so that you call attention to yourself.

Child: Hey, this is scary. I don't think I want to date.

Parent: Well, that's like saying I'm never going to talk to anyone. Of course you are. But you should know people before you go off with them. And you should know them very well. You can't help being overpowered. But you *can* do what you can to make sure you know a lot about the guy you are with and where you go with him.

Child: Do you have any other good news? I don't think I'll sleep tonight.

Parent: Look, I'd rather have you live in a world where everybody was safe and happy. And most of the time it is that way. And just as you can enjoy the good times, and should, so you've got to take care that there are as many good times as possible. You have to take care that your world is as good as you can make it. That's why we talked to you about rape. It's because we love you and want you to be okay.

Child: Yeah, I know. But it's really gross.

As we think about the figures we have seen on date rape, we slowly realize that the dating game may be too dangerous a game. The traditional coquettish female playing hard to get with a panting male chasing after her can lead to sorry consequences. Think of the commonly held myths: Women love to be overpowered; women love to be overcome by a strong male; women really, at some level, enjoy being raped. Couple those myths with others such as: Men have to have *it* at least six times a week or they go mad; men always want more sex than women; once men get aroused, they can't stop; if they do, they suffer horribly. With these thoughts accepted, we are blinded by pretty farfetched ideas about men and women. Given this mythology, it's no wonder that an amazing number of young men admitted to date rape but then went on to say, "I really thought when she said no that she didn't mean it. There was no way I could have known." If "no" is then heard as enticing and provocative, then clearly we have to provide different information to our young ones.

Actually, if you have taught your children from the time they were little that their bodies are theirs and that no one may touch them in a way they don't like, your work is almost complete. That message becomes an easy springboard to saying to your children:

> "You don't ever have to let anyone do anything to your body that you won't want. That goes all the way from touching to hitting to sex. Your 'no' should be loud and firm. Your actions should match your words: Push away, leave the scene, scream. Take care of yourself."

And your sons should hear that one way to show respect for another would be respecting that person's feelings about her body. Pay attention to what the person says and abide by it.

Of course, you want your children to learn to love in a sexual way, but with respect, responsibility, and caring.

As you can see from these dialogues, we want to help you inform your children for their own safety, to assure them that they have your love and support all the way. And we also want them to know that they are responsible for seeing to it that they do all they can do to keep themselves safe, too. They operate as your partners in being well and happy. As parents you will do what you can. Encourage them to do what they can, too. As partners in such a venture, you can be trusting, warm, and intimate with your children and they with you. and that's what we call a happy ending.

CHAPTER SIX

The Terrible Ifs

As we begin our final chapter we want first to summarize some of the parenting principles we have been endorsing throughout this book, and then go on to deal with what we call "the terrible ifs." Our reasoning is that parents need every principle they can find to handle those, and a recap might be appropriate here.

Loving Your child

It is pretty clear that we have stressed *showing* your love to your children. Obviously, you love your children—otherwise you would not be reading these words. Sometimes, however, some parents need to give themselves permission to make that love clearly evident to their children. Some parents are afraid that showing love might "spoil" their children. Others are afraid that the children will take their parents' love for granted and reason that they are loved anyway, so why bother doing what they are told? We don't find that to be the rule in the families with whom we have worked. Love, freely expressed, is always good.

Respecting Your Child

Our next principle has been showing respect for your child. Perhaps this is better stated in an expanded form: showing your respect for your child's individuality and capacity for normal development. It does not mean respecting your child's decision that she will stay home and play today rather than go to school. You might respect her *wish* to do that, just as you might your own wish to stay home and not go to work today. But, despite her wish, if all is normal, you send her firmly off to school, knowing that setting limits and requiring good behavior are not tantamount to disrespect.

Respecting your child means that if your child is not interested in Little League, although most kids in the neighborhood are, you respect his wish to do something else. It means that if your daughter is not interested in joining Girl Scouts but prefers to devote herself to her hamsters, that's o.k. In that way you show your respect for your child's preferences.

Being Straightforward with Your Child

We feel you could do a better job of being straightforward if you knew your own history and values, because knowing yourself is the first step to accepting yourself. Once you accept who you are, you can stand right there and tell your child (or the world) what you want. And you don't have to make any excuses for it. One of the side effects is that your child will find life much simpler if she knows that you present yourself clearly and firmly. Parents who waffle on their positions often create an opportunity for children to manipulate.

Being Available to Your Child

Being available means being ready to help your child with problems, doubts, and—most important of all—with feelings. It also means, as many of our illustrations have shown, sharing your own experiences and feelings with your child. We have often referred to the value of self-revelation—one of the most powerful ways of being available.

Nurturing the Self-Respect of Your Child

You may have always known but never really thought about the fact that the self is made up of two parts: body and behavior. When you think of "yourself," you may be referring to your body, parts of which you may like or not. The rest of you is how you behave, your personality. Your self-respect is the sum of your opinion of these two parts of you.

If you respect your child, and show your respect for yourself in being straightforward, then the message of self-respect will get through easily. Children learn by following the model set by their parents and teachers. Your kids learn more from what you do than from what you say. Your self-respect begets their self-respect.

Perhaps one of the earliest ways of nurturing self-respect, which we demonstrated previously, was in talking about that fine body that you want your little ones to describe accurately with the right words. You also may recall that we have urged you to praise your child for something good that she does—like saying hello to visitors at the door. Encourage your kids to feel good about their bodies and their behavior by praising both when they deserve it. That will nurture self-respect.

Holding Your Child Responsible for Her Choices

If your healthy daughter chooses not to do her homework, don't give her a note for the teacher saying she was ill and should be excused. Let her be responsible for her choices. That's an easy example. Let's make it tougher. What if the teacher says that anyone who doesn't hand in homework on time cannot attend the prom? Now we'll make it really tough. Suppose your daughter has a date for the prom, has purchased a new dress for the occasion with money she has earned? Now what?

You might be tempted to talk to the teacher or the principal, or write the note. We hope you'd let your daughter work it out with the teacher any way she could. That's one of the times that parenting is really hard for most of us. We want our children to have fun, but we don't want them to be manipulative.

Disagreeing or Disapproving in a Way That Leaves Your Child in No Doubt about Your Opinion but Leaves Her Self-Esteem Intact

That's a long title, and it says just about all there is to say. It goes along with being straightforward with your child, and with nurturing her self-respect.

It presents us with an opportunity to talk about "I" statements, however, which work very well in demonstrating this principle. It's appropriate to say to a child who has done something you dislike or disapprove of:

> "I really think you made a bad choice. I can't imagine why you did that. I hope you don't do that again. I abhor such actions . . ." etc.

Please note that the statement begins with "I" and not "*you*." When we use the pronoun "I" we are speaking for ourselves. We are not pointing fingers or putting down as we do if we begin with "you." For example, note the difference between the following two statements:

- I am shocked that you would put the cat in the toilet. What a dreadful thing to do!
- Your behavior is disgusting. You are gross. You can't be trusted.

Look at the difference: In the first example we establish boundaries—this is what you did. I don't like what you did, but our relationship is still there. You're capable of doing better, and I will help you in any way that I can because I am still invested in you.

In the second statement, you've made it clear you think your child is a bad kid. The implications are that she is a bad kid through and through, with no hope. In a way, she has been written off. There is no room for improvement. Once a jerk, always a jerk.

Your Child Is Gay

With these principles in mind, let's look at some terrible ifs. Let's suppose that your teenage child informs you that he's gay or she's a lesbian. We're going to use "he" from now on to avoid clumsiness but, once again, what we say holds for either sex. It's okay to feel what you feel at a time like this. It's okay to share your feelings. You'd be less than human if you didn't. Be aware, however, that the usual reaction to anything unpleasant is denial.

> "I can't believe it. You don't mean it. Is this a joke? How do you know? You've got to see a therapist. This is just a phase you're going through. You'll come to your senses. I know you will."

Now, how much of that can you share with your child? All of it. You haven't put him down. You've expressed your shock. That's an appropriate thing to do.

And it's certainly all right to share your disappointment. It's not what you dreamed of for your child as you paced the hall with him when he was an infant. It's certainly not what you had in mind when you cheered him on through Little League.

> "I had no idea. I am shocked. I am so troubled and disappointed. I wish it would all go away. It's so much easier to be normal. I fear for the life you have chosen."

Of course, you must express your feelings using "I" statements. If we level with our children about our feelings, then they know they can trust us.

It might be helpful at this point to increase our understanding about homosexuality. Feelings are often eased by facts, so let's take a look at some of those facts as we understand them.

Is Homosexuality a Disease?

Learning that your child is or may be homosexual is one of the most difficult things for parents to deal with. It's an overwhelming realization because it changes so much that you may have taken for granted: marriage, a new child-in-law, and grandchildren are but a few of those dashed expectations. Hopes crash and dreams die with a finality akin to death. We have worked with many families and individuals who have had to face this gigantic change, and have seen the suffering that results for even the most liberal, modern, sophisticated families who have accepted homosexuality in their friends and in society at large.

"Different" is a good word to describe homosexuality, because it does not imply sickness. Homosexuality is not an illness, and recent changes in accepted psychiatric diagnoses have indicated that. Homosexuals are neither sick nor crazy. They are not suffering from a disease that can be cured by medication. Nor are they suffering from a psychological state that can be "cured" by therapy in the way that therapy can alleviate anxiety or depression.

Another, more difficult, concept is that homosexuality is not generally a matter of will. At least, we have not seen that to be the case in our practice over the last twenty-five years, nor have any practitioners we know of. Think of it this way: If we are heterosexual, we could no more *will* ourselves to practice homosexuality as our permanent lifestyle than a homosexual can will himself to practice heterosexuality. The reason we have used the word "generally" is because there are, of course, isolated instances of a more or less homosexual nature that occur in many of our lives. And there are variations of homosexuality. It is not always an exclusive lifestyle; many people are bisexual and enjoy sex with either male or female partners. Others are asexual, desiring to avoid sexual experiences of any kind.

We have included this explanation to help soften the

blow. We suggest that you accept the idea that your child is not being wickedly willful but is experiencing a change that may have been with him at birth, or may have developed from causes that we frankly do not as yet understand. Some of our gay clients have told us that when they think back, they have known they were different since the age of five. Others have reported a gradually developing realization of their sexuality. Many have resisted that change vigorously. Many are deeply unhappy that they are homosexual, and many are proud of their sexuality and regard it as a declaration of individual freedom to be what they are.

Please note that we have *not* discussed morality. That is a private value judgment that we all must make for ourselves.

Can Parents Look for Their Homosexual Children to Change to Heterosexuality?

The answer is a difficult one, but it has been our experience that change is rare—not totally impossible, but infrequent. The pattern just does not seem to "go away." Even those who resent their homosexuality and would prefer the straight life find it difficult to live that way. Many have come to us for help to make this change, and have ended their therapy accepting their lot reluctantly.

What does this mean for the parents who want to do the most they can to encourage change? It means, in two words, *don't push*. Let your child clearly know your preferences and your feelings. Express them gently, firmly, and with love for your child, and then—stop. We suggest you avoid pressure, because there is always the remote possibility that your child is using sexual difference as a way to be different from you, to get your attention, or to test your capacity to accept him or her. If that is the case, pressure may beget a hardening of his behavior in response to you.

What about therapy for your child? Offer it, by all means,

but, as we suggested above, realize that therapy will be more likely to provide needed self-acceptance than it is to cause change. Therapy may facilitate change if that is possible, however. We recommend family therapy as well as individual treatment for several reasons. Family therapy eliminates the notion that the homosexual family member is the "sick one," helps all members of the family deal out in the open with this adjustment, and helps maintain the family as a unit so that homosexuality does not break it apart. Rejection and isolation do nothing for change.

Maintaining the Relationship

Perhaps the most useful and satisfying goal when dealing with a homosexual child proves to be maintaining the relationship. Banishment has worked out poorly. It does not help the child and, in the long run, becomes inordinately painful for the parents. Accepting your child's homosexuality is one of those decisions with no real "happy" resolution possible, but some resolutions are less painful than others. It is like going through divorce or sending a loved one to a nursing home: It may be better but it is not best.

Remember that there are usually more members of the family than just you as parents. If you banish your child, brothers and sisters may miss him terribly and blame you. Cousins, aunts, and uncles may have more tolerance and may secretly continue their relationship—causing a separation between them and you. The ramifications are wide-ranging and generally destructive.

Be aware, though, that maintaining the relationship with your child may not be easy. You may be asked to meet your child's lover, to invite him to your home, or to be a guest at the couple's home. That may be difficult, but it is amazing how your feelings can change when you contemplate losing your child instead.

If we may be permitted to cite a few examples: We have seen families go into mourning over the "loss" of their child, we have seen parents suffer severe depression, and we have seen angry parents strutting with pride at their firm and final rejection of their child. And we have also seen families accepting their child's companion as they would accept a friend or roommate, with a place set for him at holiday times and family celebrations. One more point: Difficult as it may be for parents to accept, a homosexual relationship can be one of lasting love and of loving difficulties, the same as any heterosexual relationship. Gay people have similar fights and similar differences. They even find that sexual similarity does not mean sexual compatibility. They frequently benefit from sex education and sex therapy. And when they grow older, they sometimes have difficulty parenting their children from a previous marriage, if that has been their history.

Thus we come back to some old values in a new situation. Maintain the same values with your homosexual child that you have previously shown for healthy living and a caring life style. Foster responsibility—to himself and to his associates. Foster healthy limit-setting, and model this by setting your own limits. And do what you can for yourself. Look for a support group for parents of homosexuals, and join it. Learn all you can about homosexuality from books, courses, and discussion groups. If you have trouble locating resources, do not hesitate to contact the gay group resources in your community and ask what they have to offer parents.

Do all of this within your own value system. All we are recommending is some new learning; we don't recommend that you give up and give in.

Talking to Your Homosexual Children

No matter how accepting or troubled you are, you have an obligation to talk to your homosexual children about their relationships. The same interpersonal rules that we have explored for heterosexual couples apply for homosexual couples as well.

Let's suppose that your seventeen-year-old son Tim has told you that he's gay. It had never occurred to you that homosexuality could ever be a possibility, so you were totally unprepared for the disclosure. At first you argued that it couldn't be so. Then when the initial shock wore off, you faced your anger and disappointment. You kept the anger to yourselves: "It isn't your fault he is gay; it isn't his fault he is gay." So your anger is really directed at fate for dealing you a tough hand. Tim can't help that. Neither can you. But you can voice your concern and disappointment in ways we had suggested earlier. Do not be ashamed to cry and to hug.

Then settle down to explore in the following way:

Parent: You know, Tim, relationships between people, regardless of their sexual preferences, follow the same rules.

Tim: What do you mean?

Parent: Well, let's look at it this way—no one, lesbian or gay or straight, wants to be hurt. Everyone wants to be treated responsibly and caringly. Because you have chosen a sexual style different from many people's doesn't mean you have the right to take advantage of anyone or, for that matter, let anyone take advantage of you. Being homosexual doesn't change who you are. You deserve caring and trust just as we hope you can provide it.

Tim: Thanks. I knew that but it feels good to hear you say it.

Parent: Good. You're still our son and we love you. We still wish you weren't gay, but I suppose you wish we were different in some ways, too.

Tim: Nah—you're okay.

Parent: Well, we're glad to hear that. But there's more we need to say. We're very concerned that you pick a partner who is capable of loyalty and commitment. We are convinced that promiscuity leads to nothing

| | but emptiness. You cheat yourself out of the joy that a profound relationship provides. |

Tim: Okay, okay.

Parent: Then there's another thing we need to talk about, and that's your sexual safety.

Tim: Look, I can take care of that.

Parent: Can you? That's great to hear, but we need to tell you that AIDS is fatal and that herpes or any other STD is no fun. You must take care of yourself.

Tim: Look, I know all about condoms and AIDs. We hear about it in school.

Parent: Great! Then you know about the danger of anal sex?

Tim: Hey what is this?

Parent: Well, this is the same discussion we've had with your older brother and sister when they were starting to be sexually active. There's no difference. We feel it is each person's responsibility to take care of his body. Careful, responsible choices of partners and prophylactics and careful sexual practices are the way to go. Remember, you're in charge of you.

Tim: Yeah, well, don't worry. I sure don't want AIDS. Or any other disease. I have to go now. I have basketball practice, okay?

Parent: Sure, we'll talk again.

As in previous dialogues, you've provided information, stressed responsibility for health, shared your love and desire that your child be a caring partner. And, of course, you've indicated that he is responsible for his choices and whatever happens to him.

What About "Coming Out"?

"Coming out" means someone announcing to family and friends that he is gay or that she is a lesbian. Some homosexuals feel that they need to explain their sexual inclination to their family and friends. Others prefer to remain silent.

Some families are open and share their news. Others are closed and prefer privacy. Each family acts in accordance with its own values; there is no right or wrong way. If your child acts in a manner parallel to the family values, there is apt to be less trauma for the family; in other words, the open family does better tolerating coming out, and the closed family does better with secrecy and even denial.

However, if your child announces his intention to come out in a way inconsistent with family values, then we might suspect that he is expressing some anger and revolt. His action will shock and hurt the family. Perhaps the best way to handle such serious feelings is to consult with a family therapist who can help the family understand the underlying problems and resolve them before serious pain has been inflicted.

Let's make this discussion more alive and relevant by putting together some of our experiences in the form of a "case history." We had been working with a family that had been badly split some three years prior to their visits with us. There had been a bitter divorce: The mother, let's name her Louise, was a solid, devoted, realistic woman. She radiated wholesomeness. We called her "earth mother" because of her fundamental and sound value system. She had inordinate patience until you went past her limits and then—watch out—you were dismissed from her life. That was what caused the divorce. After years of her husband's inadequate parenting and "spousing," Louise discovered that her husband, Andy, had had an affair, and she divorced him. He went off to live with this paramour who, of course, was twenty years younger than he. Louise got the ramshackle old house. He got married.

Three years later Andy asked for all to join in family therapy. Why? Because Andy had learned that his Louise, whom he'd found plain, had found a very un-plain, tall, older man who was gentle, loving, and rather well off. He had moved into the ramshackle old house and was restoring it, room by room. He was a contractor who restored whole city blocks, and this was a nice little project for him. His name was Pasquale, he was very Italian, and he was very much in love with Louise. She reminded him of his wife, who had died twelve years earlier. For reasons that all divorced parents understand, Andy was very upset with all of this.

Stuart, the oldest of their three children, is the central character in our portion of this story. He had just turned eighteen and was in the beginning of his senior year of high school. He had been held back a year because of learning difficulties that had surfaced before the divorce. He was a gentle young man, an early political, liberal activist, and rather quiet. He often seemed depressed. He was very close to his mother and had been her resource for years.

When Pasquale came into the family, Stuart welcomed him. Louise was surprised, because she expected Stuart to resent the intrusion. Stuart explained:

Stuart: Mother, I always wanted you to have someone who gave you what you deserve. Dad didn't do it, and I resented him for that.

Louise: I know, Stuart, and I think you often tried to make up for his omissions.

Stuart: No, I couldn't do that, I just sort of tried to help. Now Pasquale helps and seems to enjoy doing it.

Louise: I'm afraid, dear, that I didn't realize how much I relied on you until Pasquale did come into my life. But I don't want you to feel that now that I have him, I no longer appreciate you. I don't want you to feel displaced or replaced—you know what I mean.

Stuart: Mom, I am not jealous. It's something else . . .

Louise: What something else? What do you mean?

Stuart: For now, what I mean is hard to say. It's hard to tell you that I am relieved that you have an adult male lover. It's hard for me to tell you that I am relieved of the load— yeah, the load—of being a woman's emotional support.

Louise: It's okay. It's okay for you to say that, Son.

Stuart: I'm not copping out, Mom. It's not that. It's that I'm eighteen and I need to go live my own life, in my own way. I've got to split, Mom, someday, you know—and having Pasquale here makes it easier. I've got to say that.

Louise: Stuart, I don't think you are a selfish brat, I really don't. Of course you have to live your own life.

Stuart: But, Mom, that might not be so easy, it might not be as easy as you think, not at all as easy, Mom.

That conversation took place in the course of family therapy. Stuart had asked for a meeting with his mother alone, after the second family meeting. Let's take another look at what was said, with the added knowledge (as he told us later) that he was struggling with new, growing feelings of homosexuality.

We saw that Stuart immediately let Louise know that he disapproved of his father's treatment of her and that he was not trying to make up for Dad's "omissions." We know now, that he included "sexual omissions"—the loving, heterosexual sexuality that Stuart could not feel. Of course, Stuart's notions were combined with a normal incest taboo: Sons aren't supposed to have sex with their mothers. But Stuart had a special, added problem.

Stuart's denial of jealousy is real: He is eighteen, he knows what love means, and he is the kind of loving kid who wants his mother to have normal sexual love with a good person. His desire to "come out of the closet," to share with his mother the kind of love he feels by telling her he wants to live his life in his own way is the first hint she gets. It's touching because he has shown her how liberal he is in permitting her to love as she sees fit; now he begins to test and see if she can accept him.

A few weeks later he did just that. He told her he was gay and that he had a lover. Louise was not surprised; she had been aware that he was not dating and that he did not socialize much. She was also aware of the deep hostility Stuart felt toward his father for abandoning the family.

That was quite real: Andy had had a number of affairs, culminating in his affair with a much younger woman. Louise knew Stuart judged that to be more lust than love. In addition, Andy had fought hard in court to get the lowest possible support payments he could, and then was constantly late and short in his payments. Louise had gone to work, and Stuart was left to do all he could to help with the house and his younger siblings. The latest rejection had been Andy's refusal to help Stuart with tuition for the training school he had chosen. Louise therefore felt that Stuart could not stand another parental rejection and that she had to accept him and stand by him.

We are telling you about this complicated case because like everything in life homosexuality does not occur in a vacuum. It's one thing to make abstract recommendations about the problem of discovering your child is gay. It is quite another when, like Louise, you find yourself torn by your own feelings; your new sexual relationship outside of marriage; a child justifiably hostile at being abandoned by one parent; your first job, worrying about children home after school without your being there, and secretly wishing you could take your lover and flee the country! This was not what Louise had planned for herself at forty-four.

A few days later, Stuart made an appointment to see the male therapist alone. He needed to talk "man to man." He told about his conversation with his mother and asked for some individual therapy to help him deal with his feelings about homosexuality. After a few meetings he decided to tell his father, and wondered where and how he might do that. He worked hard, exploring how his dad might react, how he should conduct himself if Andy were accepting, or angry, or hysterical. He and his therapist tried to anticipate everything. They role-played; they switched roles; they put themselves on videotape and critiqued the playbacks; they did everything they could imagine.

Stuart's choice was to invite his father to come to our office and to tell him there. We have a "safe space" concept that we always explain to our clients, and Andy was well aware of it. We suggest that safe space means, of course, no physical violence or destruction of property, and it also means that you may say anything, or nothing; you may answer questions, or elect to "pass." In addition, if there is too much pressure for you, you may leave the room but agree to stay in the building, and in five minutes or so, give us a knock on the door and let us know that you are okay. Stuart felt that this would provide a setting in which he would have a better chance of a productive talk with his father.

Why all this preparation? Stuart was angry, afraid, and hostile, of course. But there were other factors of tremendous impact. Stuart, like all children, wanted to love his father, and wanted his father to deserve that love—to be someone a son could be proud of! And of course, he wanted his father to be proud of him, and he knew that Andy was highly unlikely to be proud of his homosexuality. After all, Andy's chasing after women was exaggerated evidence of the exact opposite—a kind of overemphasis on heterosexuality, a defensive, inappropriate pursuit of sex.

Our concern as therapists and parents, however, was: Is Stuart "using" this occasion to get back at his father, to hurt him where he is most vulnerable, to dramatize the exact opposite of his father's failing? Does he want to hurt his father with the exact symbolic opposite action that father "used" to hurt Stuart? Is Stuart saying: "Okay, Dad, if you want to play rough with the family, using sex as your weapon, I'll show you a rough move that will shake your sexual values deeper than you shook ours!"

Let's take that concern one step further—the ultimate step. Did Stuart *become* homosexual as a response to his father's behavior? And to generalize that question, let us ask: Do children sometimes develop homosexuality in response to their surroundings? Frankly we do not know the answer to that question, and we doubt that anyone else does, either. And since that answer is unknown, we suggest that all parents who discover their children are gay try tentative testing and exploration rather than automatic anger and rejection.

How did Stuart's meeting with his father turn out? It turned out to be bland and empty because Andy used his usual first pattern of defense, which should be pretty clear to us by now. He withdrew again. It went something like this:

When they came into the office, Andy made the first move, hoping to get an alliance with the adult therapist.

Andy: What's this all about? Stuart asked me to come and I suppose he's afraid to ask me alone about something. I can't do much more, Doc. I can't support two house-holds, there have to be some limits—I love this kid but I can't do anything more.

The therapist, who was trying very hard to avoid making any alliance, mumbled something unintelligible and looked at Stuart. It worked: Stuart responded and father and son were on their own from that point on, and in a safe space.

Stuart: Dad, I didn't ask you here to get anything material from you. I just don't want to hurt you and I just need you to know—about me, that is. That's all.

Andy: What do you mean, "hurt me"? And I know you're mad about school tuition, and I feel bad about that but it does not hurt me. It saddens me; I wish I could help more. Look, maybe I can help with a loan. I'll sign for you—how much more can I do?

Stuart: Dad, that's not it, not it at all. Dad, I need you to just listen for a while. Would that be okay with you, really, Dad? Would you just listen for a while?

Andy: You sound like this is very important to you, Stuart. Yes, I'll listen. Go ahead.

Stuart: Dad, you have often urged me to go out on dates with girls. You have offered me the car and things—you've been okay, you really have.

Andy: Yeah—so . . .

Stuart: Dad, you said you would listen. Please, Dad . . .

Andy: All I said was, "Yeah, so . . ." So I'll be quiet. Wasn't that all I said, Doc?

"Doc" didn't take the bait, and he concentrated on his shoelace.

Stuart: You have to know the reason why I have not been dating, Dad. It goes pretty deep and it is hard to tell you this but I'd better say it straight out: I'm gay, Dad.

There was a dead silence while Andy looked first at his son and then at the therapist. His eyes filled with tears, but his voice was steady:

Andy: I heard you, Stu, I heard you and I often hoped I never would hear that, but you've been sort of telegraphing it for some time. Are you sure? Do you have to be sure— you do have to be sure, don't you? How do you know for sure?

Stuart: I just know. It seems strange, I suppose, but somehow you just know. Sort of like you just know when you love someone.

Andy: That's pretty adult talk for an eighteen-year-old kid. Maybe someday when this is all over, maybe you'll feel different, maybe.

Stuart: Dad, you don't seem angry.

Andy: What's to be angry? I'm sad, not angry. And maybe I still got hope, you know. There is always hope. I've known lots of guys who thought they were qu————, gay, you call it. They're okay now. Maybe this is just a phase—maybe it's you who's angry with me, huh?

Stuart: I don't know if that's it.

Andy: Have you told your mother? Does she know?

Stuart: She knows. And I don't suppose she feels any better about it than you do.

Andy: She knows! How could you tell her a thing like that? Why did you do that?

Stuart:	For the same reason I'm telling you, Dad.
Andy:	For the same reason, huh? I'll never understand that reason. I'll never understand this, or you—I don't know . . . what the hell is a father supposed to say at a time like this? What the hell am I supposed to do? Is this my fault or something? Doc—what am I supposed to do?
Therapist:	Andy, actually you *are* doing all you can. And you listened, and that was good. The only thing I suggest you do is to hang in there. Keep talking to your son. Don't split.
Andy:	Well, I can't listen anymore now, no more now. Stuart, you've got to live your own life. I can't help you with this one. Tuition—yes, come talk to me. I'll always talk to you—but I can't help with this. I don't see how I can.

Andy left the room. A few minutes later he came back and said he would rather end the visit right there. Stuart agreed, of course.

We talked a bit after father left. Stuart said that he was disappointed, of course, with the outcome of the meeting but that he had known it could happen that way. He was glad he had tried. We talked about whether he was reaching out to his father with a dramatic appeal for understanding, or confronting his father with his failure as a parent. Or was he doing both?

| Stuart: | I suppose I was doing all of those things, and more besides. I guess maybe what you said jokingly once is not such a joke. I think you said something about children are doomed to fail to bring their parents up properly. That's about it. |

If Your Child Is Raped

Another terrible *if* is rape . . . for either your son or your daughter. Certainly it's nothing any of us wants to think about, and fortunately not many of us have to, but since rape does occur, let's look at what are some of our options. As we do so, we are going to use "she" to avoid clumsiness, but please note that what we say applies to either our sons or daughters.

Keep in mind that it is easy for the victim to become demoralized. The victim internalizes the injury and insult and decides that somehow she is to blame. After a crime like this, the last thing we want is for our child to feel guilt. She has enough healing to do without adding unnecessary burdens. Many girls report that they felt responsible in some way:

> "If I had been a different kind of person, he never would have done that to me. Somehow it was my fault. I am so deeply ashamed."

> "Maybe if I hadn't—worn a tight dress, walked alone . . ." [You can fill in the blanks any way you want.]

All of this may be real to the victim but none of it is the way you want your daughter to feel. What you *do* want her to feel is anger. You also want her to feel good about herself, to know that the rapist was evil, and that she is innocent and good.

So the best thing parents can do is comfort and reassure:

> "My darling child, thank God you're alive. Let me hug and hold you. Whatever happened, you're still my beautiful, precious child. Don't ever forget that! I'm so proud of you for getting through it and surviving. I don't know how you did it. But I know you're some kind of heroine. What guts you've got! I hate hearing about this, but I'm glad you came to me and told me. I want to be there for you. Naturally we have to make sure you're all right. We'll see that you have a medical checkup as soon as possible."

Of course, it's also natural for you to feel anger, horror, and revulsion toward the rapist. By all means, share that with your child. Those words will come to you easily. We don't have to supply them. Encourage your child to voice *her* loathing and horror, also. The best thing for her is to convert her shame to anger.

Whatever you may privately feel, this is not the time for blame. As we said, it's the time for hugs, reassurance, and congratulations for having survived such an ordeal. It's not the time to say something like:

> "I warned you that if you wore all that makeup and those short skirts you'd be in trouble."

> "I warned you you'd get in trouble if you kept going out with that gang. But you never listened to me. Now maybe you'll see I was right."

> "Maybe now you'll pay attention to what I've been telling you about modesty and careful behavior. Next time you won't be so lucky. You'll be dead!"

Even if you're right, don't say it. What your daughter needs to know is that under no circumstances does she deserve such treatment. The rapist is always wrong and the victim is always right.

Your next task is to get your child to a hospital where there is a rape counselor available. There she can be medically checked for any injuries or possible STDs or pregnancy. Hospital officials can also gather evidence to use in court, should you and your daughter decide to prosecute. A trained rape counselor can be sensitive and helpful. She can reinforce your efforts to assure your daughter that she was in no way to blame. Then, too, someone who has been raped may find it easier to talk with counselors about the specifics of the crime. Finding that she can talk about the rape to another sympathetic person, without criticism or rejection, is comforting and helps restore her damaged self-esteem.

The rape counselor can also help the family decide what to do about prosecuting the rapist. Talking to the police and giving evidence in court are difficult issues for most women, both old and young. Many report that they feel that it is more humiliating to go through a court appearance than it is just to live with what happened. Teenage girls, in particular, tell us that they can't stand the idea of going back to school and having classmates talk about it. They're sure that girls will tease them and that boys will cease to respect them. Often they're convinced that whatever popularity they had will vanish with disclosure. They worry, they tell us, in the following ways:

> "I'm so afraid every boy will think I'm ready for sex and more violence. I don't know if I have the right to say no, and if I do, what boy will listen to me? The girls won't have any respect for me, either. Bet their parents will think I'm some sort of bad influence and won't let them be with me. And what will my teachers think of me? Bet they'd all be laughing behind my back. It's too much! I can't take any more chances."

Since these feelings are so strong, it seems to us that as parents you must explore alternatives with your daughter, but let her make the final decision about prosecuting. You may feel strongly that she either should or should not prosecute but, in either event, *she* is the one to decide what is right for her. If you try to talk her into doing what you think is right, you may be telling her subtly that she doesn't know what she is doing. Her self-esteem is already badly shaken; arguing against what she thinks is right for her may confirm to her that she isn't worthy of making any kind of judgment. Then her self-esteem drops even more. Respecting her opinion and abiding by it encourages her to see that she is still worthwhile. You are telling her that what she feels is okay and what she does is okay, too. Providing that kind of reassurance is more important than any other kind of action we may take.

The last thing we want is for our children to see themselves as victims, because then they start acting like victims—afraid to assert themselves, afraid to demand their rights, just plain afraid.

Of course, it is possible that your daughter will want to prosecute. Then you will encourage her to do so and be prepared to support her all the way. That means finding sympathetic lawyers, attending conferences, and staying in court with her. Your major task will be to encourage and support as much as you can.

Now let's look at another complication. Let's suppose that you're divorced. Your daughter lives with you and sees Dad on the weekends. Your daughter tells you, Mother, that she has been raped but asks you not to tell Dad. Now what do you do? Suppose you feel strongly that, as a matter of principle, her father has the right to know what has happened to his daughter. Do you argue with your daughter? Do you ignore her and act on your principle? It's a difficult call, but once again, it seems to us, it may be better to respect your daughter's feelings and show her that you do respect her decision. Of course, this only holds if she decides not to prosecute. Naturally you would share with her your own preference, as well as noting your compliance with her wishes.

> "I would prefer you tell Dad about it. I feel very uncomfortable keeping such a secret from him. But you're the one I'm most concerned about. If you feel you can't tell him, and you don't want me to, then you won't and I won't. It will be just between us. But I do hope that you change your mind. You don't have to do it now. But think about it. It will be your decision."

If your daughter does decide to tell her father, and her brothers if she has any, we can think of nothing more reassuring than having familiar, loving, muscular arms hugging and patting, and masculine voices of support:

> "You're my lovely daughter and I love you."

> "Hey, sis, you're all right."

In summary, your job in this case is to help your child through this ordeal by helping maintain her integrity and self-respect. You will see to it that she gets medical attention, and then aid her in deciding what step to take next. But that will always be her decision. She is in charge. If she knows you think she's okay, then she'll *be* okay, and the relationship among all of you will be very good.

We have talked about how to talk with your daughter and what steps to take, and we have looked at some contingencies. There is still the emotional reaction to deal with. As parents, you may find yourselves overwhelmed with rage and a host of other feelings. You may need your own reassurance during this time, as well as a safe place to blow off steam. There's nothing wrong with getting your own counselor to talk to. The rape counselor may be able to recommend someone, or perhaps your family doctor can. There's no logical reason for you as parents to feel guilty, but sometimes you may. You may be assailed by a torrent of "If onlys": "If only I hadn't let her go out." "If only I'd said no." And so on. It can be very helpful to work out some of this anguish with a sensitive, experienced person. You can be much more helpful if you are at peace.

In addition, there is the emotional reaction that any traumatized person experiences. For a period of time, almost all victims of unexpected violence report regular nightmares and flashbacks. In her nightmares, your daughter will relive the rape scene, and in flashbacks, which occur during waking hours, she will suddenly find herself reviewing what happened to her. Although people are distressed by the nightmares and impatient with the flashbacks, be assured that it's normal to experience them; it's all part of the healing process. The nightmares and flashbacks may continue for weeks and even months. That's the way nature helps us heal—by having us relive the terror until we can tolerate it and make peace with it, and then get on with our lives. So if your daughter complains about these phenomena, reassure her that they're normal, if unpleasant, and that it is good that she is experiencing these symptoms because they are a sign of improving health.

You will probably also find her nervous and jumpy. That, too, is a natural reaction to a stressful event. What she needs is as much support and sympathy as you can provide. She needs to know that she is normal, and that she will get through it.

Let's suppose that you find that your daughter is afraid to date again. We think it makes no sense to push her, hoping that she'll forget the whole episode sooner. It's better to respect her time schedule for healing. Since we are all so different, it's impossible to say how long it will take for anyone to regain confidence, both in herself and others. Sometimes, in an effort to be helpful, we urge people to get on with their lives before they are ready to do so. Doing so may inadvertently set up an adversarial position. Your daughter may read it as another sign that what she feels is neither good nor right. It's better to be understanding:

> "Yes, I know. You're probably still uncomfortable being around young people. That will pass with time. Don't worry. We have all the confidence in the world in you. You're okay."

If, however, you feel your daughter is stuck, she would undoubtedly benefit from therapy. If she can get into a group for young women who have also been raped, her progress will be much faster. It's immeasurably comforting to know that you're not unique, that others have gone through similar crises, and have survived and continued with their lives. Feeling normal and trusting is what recovery is all about. With the support of an understanding family and good friends, and therapy if needed, she can successfully rebuild her life.

If Your Child Becomes Pregnant or is Responsible for a Pregnancy

The last terrible *if* we are going to explore is teenage pregnancy. Although we hope that a child to whom we have talked about sex and responsibility is not going to get pregnant or cause a pregnancy, we know it might happen. We'll suppose here that your fifteen-year-old daughter comes to you, tells you that she is pregnant, and that her fifteen-year-old boyfriend is the father. Any parent's initial response would undoubtedly be denial.

"How do you know? Are you sure? You're too young and so is he."

You might be overcome with disappointment and anger, and even show these feelings to your daughter. We'd hope that after an initial outburst, you could fall back on the principles at the opening of this chapter, and use some "I" statements focused on your feelings and not on her character.

"I am very upset and very disappointed in you. I thought you would use better judgment. I find it hard to believe that you would allow such a thing to happen. I am distraught and very angry."

It's a great temptation at a time like this to convert "I" statements into something like the following:

"I think that you are a whore. I feel that you disgraced us. I think that what you did is absolutely disgusting."

The trick is to keep the "you" out of it. Otherwise you are back at the usual whipping:

"You really are no good. You're just as cheap as I feared."

Try to remember not to assassinate character. Your child has what you hope will be a long life ahead of her, and you want to encourage her to make more mature decisions and to act more responsibly. So once again, share with her just how you feel, but do what you can to keep her self-esteem intact. The last thing you want is for her to be discouraged about herself and think that, since there is no hope for her, it makes no difference what she does for the rest of her life.

Let us suppose that the parents are separated, and that the daughter asks her mother not to tell her father. Of course, as in any other situation, circumstances alter cases. In general, however, we recommend that her father be informed. The rationale is that your daughter will do better dealing with reality than avoiding it with secrets that are bound to come out later. Some ex-wives are afraid that their former husbands will use this kind of thing against them, to taunt them with not being good mothers. Our major concern would be that your daughter might use the situation to manipulate you, saying, "Well, I'll live with Dad. He won't care. I'd have more fun with him, anyway." Our motto is, "Where there are no secrets, there is no manipulation." But still and all, it's a judgment call.

Unluckily, with a pregnancy, no one has the luxury of time. You have to explore what your options are, and make some decisions fast. And each family must come to its own decision within the values of its own system. For example, if abortion is abhorrent to you, then that eliminates that as a solution. That might not be so for another family.

Our purpose is to help you guide your daughter through this very difficult, sensitive time. A primary concern would be to involve your daughter in the decision-making process and make her undertake her responsibilities as much as possible for whatever decision the family agrees upon. Of course, the judgment of a fifteen-year-old isn't all that great—she's just demonstrated that. On the other hand, children, like adults, are better off if they have to look at all options available to them, weigh the advantages and disadvantages, and then decide. We'd like them to taste, as it were, the consequences of their actions. Yet, we'd also want them to retain confidence in their ability to cope and to retain confidence in their relationship with us.

With these thoughts in mind, we'd mention marriage. We'd talk about abortion. We'd explore the pluses and minuses of having the baby and putting her up for adoption. There is always the possibility of having the baby and then placing the child in a foster home where your daughter and the child's father could visit the baby, stay in touch with the child until such time as they (or she, or he) are ready to take the child. Then, too, your daughter could have the child and keep her home where you, the grandparents, could, if willing, take over much of the child care. You might want to teach and coach about parenting until your daughter could take over the total responsibility of her child. Obviously, no solution is ideal, and your daughter and/or son needs to know that. As we said, your role would be as guide and resource person. But it is your daughter who must take responsibility for her choice. We would ask questions like these:

- Have you given any thought about how you are going to handle this pregnancy?
- Can your boyfriend help you with the hospital costs?
- Can your boyfriend help you support this child?
- Have you explored this with him? You will need money, you know.
- If I keep the baby for you until you are old enough to take over, will you get a job after school to help with the expenses?
- What kind of job do you think you can get? You realize, of course, that it will be important for you to maintain your school work as well. We'll do some of the babysitting but you will have to be prepared to take over most of the time. We'll negotiate what nights you can count on.

- If you decide to give the baby up for adoption, where will you spend your time until you deliver?
- Will you stay at home?
- I would like you to finish high school. You'll have to find out what the policy of the school is about having pregnant students around. '
- Since you seem to think that adoption is the best solution, can you see yourself giving up a child? Will you be able to face life knowing that somewhere you have a child who doesn't know you?"

By now, you've got the idea. By all means, be as thorough as possible, but always involve your daughter in the decision-making process and make sure that she knows that the responsibility is ultimately hers. Incidentally, should you and your daughter agree that abortion is the best solution, be sure to accompany her when she has the abortion done—it is always a lonely process and under the best of circumstances she will need lots of support. You might say something like:

"Abortion is a serious business but, if that is your choice, then I will help you with it. Together we will find a clinic, and I will go with you and stay with you. I wish this hadn't happened, but since it did, I will help you get through it in the best way that I can. People do make mistakes. Let's hope that you learn from this and exercise more good judgment the next time. I hate to see my child go through this. I know you'll be all right. I just wish it didn't have to be."

Whatever decision you reach, you should share your heartache with your daughter but, particularly in the case of abortion, we would undoubtedly share our sense of the seriousness of the act, while maintaining that she has a life ahead of her. That life can be one of promise and fulfillment, even though she has had an abortion or given birth. In other words, you would want her to know that, regardless of the past, you want her to make the most of her life, present and future. You want her to know that you will be there to help her do that in any way that you can. One of the ways to see to that is to reeducate her about the responsibility of sex and, more specifically, see to it that she really is informed about birth control.

And always, you want to make it clear that you would treasure the relationship. Remind her that when she failed to make her bed on time or didn't do her homework faithfully, you were furious and told her so. But you never abandoned her. Nor will you now. it's far from over. You love her, treasure her, and always will. She's your daughter, after all.

We have been talking about parents and their pregnant daughters, but we would urge parents of sons who have impregnated girls to follow a similar style. Hold your son responsible for what he has done; share your distress and your disappointment with him. Insist that he participate in the many decisions that have to be made, but leave him with a sense of still being worthwhile. Tell him that he still has a future in which he can act responsibly and achieve success. Fathering a child need not be the end of his world, regardless of the outcome. We suggest that you might talk to your son like this:

Parent: Tom, Susan's mother has called to say that Susan is pregnant and you are the father.

Tom: Oh, God, she told you!

Parent: There is really no excuse for this. Please understand. We're not furious because you and Susan had sex, although as we have told you we wanted you to wait until you were older. We're really furious that you weren't responsible about birth control. Now you have serious decisions to make. You're only fifteen. If Susan elects to have the baby, you have a financial obligation to that baby. That means you have to help support the child until he reaches eighteen years of age. Since every baby deserves to have a mother and father, that means you have to be emotionally involved with the child.

Tom: What do you mean?

Parent: That means you have to learn how to take care of a baby. You have to learn about the way a baby develops. You have to help your child grow into a fine, happy, healthy child. Being in charge of a child is heavy-duty stuff. You are as much responsible for the well-being of your child as Susan is.

Tom: You mean I would have to give up school and go to work? You want me and Susan to get married and live together? Geez. I don't know. What kind of a job could I get? I can't even drive. Why can't she just have an abortion?

Parent: Well, let's say that she does. How will you feel knowing that a baby you've fathered has been destroyed?

Tom: Oh geez. I don't know. I don't want to get married. I know that. Coach says I might make varsity next year. That's what I want to do. Play varsity. I could get a job weekends and help out, but I don't want to get married.

Parent: Let's finish with one topic at a time. If Susan has an abortion, you have a duty to go with her if she wants you there. You certainly should help pay for the cost of the abortion. If she decides to keep the baby, then you know what you have to do. You'd have to be financially and emotionally supportive.

Tom: Listen, it's really Susan's problem, not mine.

Parent: Wrong! You're just as involved as Susan with the well-being and care of this child, as well as any other you might father. That's what being a parent means. We agree with you. We do think you are too young to marry. But you are old enough to live with the consequences of your actions. We will be behind whatever decision you and Susan make. Remember, however, that a child is yours for as long as you live.

Tom: I had no idea!

Parent: Whether Susan keeps the baby or not, your life will be different from the other kids. You will always know that you fathered a child. That's not the end of life. It doesn't mean that you are not worthwhile. It does mean that you made a serious mistake. But your life isn't over. Not by a long shot. We're still behind you. We will expect you to be more careful in the future.

Talking to Your Children About Love and Sex

As we wrote this book we became aware that parenting exists on three levels. The first level is teaching. To teach your child, you need information. In this book we have explored the development of sexuality; we have explained the reproductive system; and we have provided information about birth control and sexual safety. In addition, we have explored ways of dealing with pregnancy, rape, and homosexuality. We have selected the sexual information that you need to teach your child about sex, love, and safety.

The second level of parenting is guiding. To guide a child you need not only information, but also values. We have stressed love, trust, intimacy, awareness of self, concern for others, respect, and responsibility. Children learn by the models their parents present. If you parents clearly understand your own values, modeling and presenting values are far more effective than merely talking about them. If you can continue to love and respect your children through their most disappointing or exasperating moments, then you have modeled for them the elasticity of love. They will learn from observation that your actions match your values. They can then incorporate your model into their own behavior.

The third level is establishing trust and intimacy with your child. To do that you need to know your sexual history and your own sexual values. You need to be comfortable enough with yourself so that you can share what is appropriate for you. Thus you model intimacy and trust. In return your children will be secure in trusting and sharing with you. The result is a warm, close, trusting relationship between you and your child. What better reward can there be?

Substitute Parents: Short- and Long-Term

Although we have written this book as a guide for parents and their children, we recognize that grandparents, other relatives, friends, and foster parents do substitute for parents under varying circumstances. We hope that anyone who is acting as a substitute parent for a long period of time has found this book helpful so far. However, for those acting as parents for a short time, there are some different considerations.

When a child is with you for a short period of time it is better to defer to the values and customs of the parents rather than to insist that the child conform to yours. Let's assume that your eight-year-old niece is visiting you for a month while her parents are traveling. Let's further suppose that the child comes from a home where modesty is a value. No one is ever unclothed in the presence of another. Since she can remember, Hilary has been instructed never to leave her room without her bathrobe on. Now she is in your home where modesty is not a factor. You and your husband are comfortable walking about in underwear or scant night clothes. Suppose Hilary complains:

Hilary: In my house everyone wears a bathrobe. My mommy and daddy say that's the way it should be.

You: In our house we act differently.

Hilary: I don't like the way you and Uncle Steve look. My mommy and daddy wouldn't like it, either. I wish I could go home.

Now what? One week down, two more to go. We would suggest that it is more important to make the child comfortable than to change her values, particularly since she will be with you for just a short time.

"Well, Hilary, we want you to feel good. So while you are here, Uncle Steve and I will try to be more modest. We don't think that modesty is right or wrong. We just want to make you happy. You be sure to remind us if we forget."

The same principle applies if, let us say, Grace, a thirteen-year-old daughter of a friend, is spending a few weeks with you and reports that Tommy, a neighbor's thirteen-year-old son, has kissed her. The best thing to do might be to ask her how her parents would feel about that. Let's say that Grace feels they wouldn't like it. Then your role is easy. Tell Grace she won't have to see Tommy again. Now let's suppose she says that her parents wouldn't care, but you're not comfortable with that. You could say something like:

"I think I don't want anything to happen that might make your mom and dad unhappy. Since I am not sure how they feel, I'm going to ask you to hold off until they get home, or until they call, and we can ask them. All right?"

Now once more let's suppose five-year-old Bobby is with you for a week. He asks you where babies come from. You are not sure how his parents would handle that, so you might tell him mommy and daddy know the answer and they will tell him when they get home. If, however, Bobby will be with you for an extended period of time, then you would answer his question as we have suggested in this book—just as you would for your own child.

Caring for another person's child is always challenging, but the same patience and flexibility that get parents through tough times will certainly be helpful for substitute parents. Be sure to give the child time to learn and adapt to your values. He may, for example, have come from a home where there was limited physical touching. You are a "touchy-feely" person. If you immediately begin hugging this child, you may find that he is pretty uncomfortable. Rather than insist, you could say:

> "Oh dear. We're so used to hugging we assume everybody likes it. We find it pleasant and loving. Maybe you will too, someday. But it's o.k. to remain apart. We'll try to respect what you like. If we forget, just tell us. We'll try to understand. But if you decide you would like a hug, just let us know."

On the other hand, if you bring a child into your home whose vocabulary is far earthier and much more explicit than you tolerate, you might say something like this:

> "There are several ways to explain something. You can use polite terms. You can use harsh terms. For example, we say we won't put up with bad behavior. You say you won't take shit from anyone. We both make our point. In this home we prefer polite talk. We're going to ask you to respect our feelings. Out of the house, with the kids, talk as you wish. Here with us, please talk our way."

The principles we have stated still hold. Respect the child and his values. Don't assassinate his character:

> "What kind of brat are you to talk that way? You've got a filthy mouth. Didn't your parents know better?"

Rather, explain what you want; assure him that he's all right. It's just that you're different. Not better. Just different. That way you are showing respect for the home he left. If you can do that, then his sense of self will be reinforced. It is much easier to get along with a child who feels good about himself and about his family. With respect in place, you're on your way to a cordial relationship in which love and sex can be explored comfortably, using the methods we have recommended.

Bibliography

Austin, Al, and Hefner, Keith, eds. *Growing Up Gay*. Ann Arbor: Youth Liberation Press, 1978.

Bell, Ruth, et al. *Changing Bodies, Changing Lives*. New York: Random House, 1980.

Benedict, Helen. *Recovery*. New York: Doubleday & Company, 1985.

Calderone, Mary S., M.D., and Ramey, James U., M.D. *Talking With Your Child About Sex*. New York: Ballantine Books, 1982.

Gitchel, Sam, and Foster, Lori. *Let's Talk about S-E-X*. Fresno, CA: Planned Parenthood of Central California, 1987.

Herman, J. L., M.D. *Father-Daughter Incest*. Cambridge, MA: Harvard University Press, 1981.

Kaplan, Helen Singer, M.D., Ph.D. *Making Sense of Sex: The Contemporary Guide for Young Adults*. New York: Simon & Schuster, 1979.

Kelly, Gary. *Learning About Sex: The Contemporary Guide for Young Adults*. Woodbury, NY: Barron's, 1976.

Ledroy, Linda, R.N., Ph.D. *Recovering from Rape*. New York: Henry Holt & Company, 1986.

Madaras, Lynda, with Saavedra, Dana. *The What's Happening to My Body Book for Boys*. New York: Newmarket Press, 1984.

Madaras, Lynda, with Madaras, Area. *The What's Happening To My Body Book for Girls*. New York: Newmarket Press, 1983.

Miklowitz, Gloria D. *Did You Hear What Happened to Andrea?* New York: Delacorte, 1979.

Oettinger, Katherine, with Mooney, Elizabeth C. *Not My Daughter: Facing Up To Adolescent Pregnancy.* New Jersey: Prentice-Hall, 1979.

Sanford, L. *The Silent Children: A Parent's Guide to the Prevention of Child Sexual Abuse.* New York: Anchor Press, Doubleday, 1980.

Silverstein, Charles. *A Family Matter: A Parent's Guide to Homosexuality.* New York: McGraw Hill, 1978.

Stewart, Felicia; Guest, Felicia, Stewart, Gary; and Hatcher, Robert. *My Body, My Health.* New York: John Wiley, 1979.

Wattleton, Faye, Pres., with Keifer, Elisabeth. *How to Talk with Your Child About Sexuality.* Garden City, NY: Planned Parenthood, Doubleday & Company, 1986.

Weisman, Betsy A., and Weisman, Michael A., M.D. *What We Told Our Kids About Sex.* New York: Harcourt Brace Jovanovich, 1987.

Index